STATE OF REVOLUTION

STATE OF REVOLUTION

*My
Seven-and-a-Half-Year
Journey Through
Revolutionary War
New Jersey*

AL FRAZZA

258 Publishing

For Toni

CONTENTS

CHAPTER 1

REVOLUTIONARY WAR NEW JERSEY

Creating the *Revolutionary War New Jersey* website was my life's big adventure. It took approximately ten-thousand hours to complete, over the course of seven-and-a-half years.

My goal was to document as much as I could about New Jersey's role in the Revolutionary War. In the process of doing so, I got to explore every corner of the state's twenty-one counties: The cities. The shore. The mountains. The farmland. The suburbs. It was an amazing experience, and I now feel privileged to have had the opportunity to explore my home state in a way that perhaps few people ever have.

In the following pages, you will hear the story of my experiences and explorations during those seven-and-a-half years. Along the way, you will also learn about some of the fascinating people I studied who lived in New Jersey during the

Revolutionary War — soldiers, officers, and statesmen, as well as farmers, ministers, and blacksmiths. Some were famous, and others were obscure, but each had a story worth learning about.

You will also hear about the interesting historic places I explored in my research: houses, buildings, churches, and cemeteries which still stand where they stood during the Revolutionary War, as well as hills, mountains, and rivers which affected the events of the war.

You will discover the important role that New Jersey played in that very important time, and see how the lives of the men and women who lived here were profoundly affected by the war.

My hope is that by reading about my own experiences, you will be inspired to go out and explore the history around you firsthand.

CHAPTER 2

BEFORE THE BEGINNING

The idea to do a *Revolutionary War New Jersey* project came to me in September, 2009. Prior to that, I had been interested in history for many years, and one of my history interests was the role of New Jersey in the Revolutionary War. Visiting historic sites had been a hobby of mine for some time, and as part of that, I had visited many Revolutionary War historic sites in New Jersey.

The more that I had learned about the important role that the state had played in the Revolutionary War, the more I became frustrated by the fact that this was not generally understood by New Jersey's own citizens, or by the rest of the country.

Over time, I found myself talking with increasing frequency about the lack of recognition of my state's role in the

Revolutionary War. Finally, in mid-September, 2009, I said to myself that it was time to either do something proactive about it, or to stop talking about it. In other words, I told myself to put up or shut up.

I decided then that I wanted to make my own contribution, but I did not know what form it would take. I thought that it would probably make the most sense for me to create a website about the topic, because designing websites was what I did for a living. But as to what the focus and scope of that website might be, I had no idea.

That day, I purchased the website domain name *revolutionarywarnewjersey.com*. But having secured the website name, I still did not know what type of website I would create for it. I figured that I would wait and see if an idea arose, and move forward if it did.

Two days later, I made the definite decision to move forward and begin to actually create the website. I still had only a very basic idea of what I wanted to do with the website, but I thought that I would figure it out as I went along.

It can sometimes be hard to look back on exactly what you were thinking at an earlier time in your life. But as best I can recall, I naively thought that whatever form the project might take, it would be something I could complete in a few months. I could not envision then how the scope of the project would continually grow and shift over time, and how much my own obsession to detail would contribute to that process.

I have often been asked if I had known at the start how long the project would take, would I have done it anyway; the honest answer to that question is NO. If I could have foreseen the years where the project would grow in size, and at times spin out of control, I would never have started it.

But fortunately, I could *not* foresee this. And so, on September 17, 2009, I found myself beginning a project which I would not complete until March 1, 2017.

CHAPTER 3

GETTING STARTED

Having made the decision to start the project, I began moving forward without a clear idea of where I was heading.

In the first few days, I came up with the basic look and design of the website, which as it turned out, I would never change. As years of work on the project passed, I would add more and more information and photos to the website, but the colors, textures, format and logo would remain essentially unchanged. Several years into the project, I would consider changing the look of the website, but by then I had become too accustomed to it. I have a great feeling for both nostalgia and tradition, as will become apparent while reading this book.

Having come up with the look of the website, I had to decide what information was to fill the pages. I began by simply listing the names and locations of historic sites which I had obtained from several books. I did not know then how much additional information to include about these locations, or how I would go about obtaining it.

I next decided to photograph all of the locations which I would list on the website. I had taken very few pictures in my life, and did not own a camera. I also did not own a smart phone (I still don't), therefore I had nothing to take the photos with. So I borrowed my Mom's digital camera to start taking the photos.

Of course, deciding to photograph all the historic sites meant having to actually drive to them. I completely and totally underestimated the enormous amount of driving this would require. (The first of many underestimations I was to make.) When you look at a map of the United States, New Jersey looks pretty tiny in comparison to large states like California, Texas, and Montana. I myself had thought of New Jersey as small before I began the project. But my perception of its size would change over the course of the next seven-and-a-half years as I made many long drives to all corners of the state to visit and photograph the Revolutionary War historic sites.

The first trip that I planned and mapped out was to photograph some Revolutionary War historic sites in Hunterdon, Warren, and Sussex Counties. The choice to start in that area was completely random as I recall. I mapped out the trip on Google Maps, which gave me an estimate that the total drive for this driving trip would take about three hours.

I thought that I could use some company and conversation on the drive, so I called my friend Paul and asked if he would like to take the drive with me. He said that he would like to see the historic sites I was going to, and agreed to take the drive.

And so with a full tank of gas and printouts of the Google Maps directions, I was ready to hit the road on my first trip.

CHAPTER 4

HITTING THE ROAD

On Saturday, September 29, 2009, twelve days into the project, I set out on my first photographing driving trip. My very first stop was the John Holcombe House in Lambertville, which George Washington had stayed at on two occasions during the war. From there, I drove on to the other historic sites I had mapped out in Hunterdon, Warren, and Sussex Counties.

It was a very nice autumn day, and the trip was an enjoyable one. Because this was my first time out, everything seemed new, and that had an excitement about it. However, several things did come up that day which in hindsight were early signs that the project might turn out to be bigger than I had imagined.

Everything Takes Longer Than Planned

As I mentioned in the previous chapter, my Google Maps directions for that first trip calculated that it should take about three hours. What I had not considered was that this estimate was only accurate if all you were doing was driving to each of the locations without stopping. However, that did not pertain to what I was actually doing.

The reality involved many things which extended the time: having to find a place to park at each location, discovering that some of my planned destinations were not located where I thought they were (or did not actually exist at all), the time taken at each stop to walk around and explore. And of course, there was the time it took to actually take the photos.

When I started the project, I had no idea how to take even decent photos of the houses, buildings, churches, and cemeteries that I visited. To compensate for this, I would take *a lot* of photos, from as many angles as I could, hoping to get some usable ones.

In the end, what had been planned as a three-hour-trip for that day ended up taking close to eight hours. And I did not even actually finish the entire trip I had planned for that day. I was getting tired of driving, and I felt bad that my friend had been kept out for much longer than he expected, so I ended up heading home before getting to the final places I had mapped out for the day.

These factors which extended the length of my drives remained pretty consistent moving forward. On average, my photographing driving trips took about three times longer than the directions alone indicated. But for some reason, for the first few years of the project, I refused to accept this reality. Through a combination of stubbornness and wishful thinking, I would insist on believing that a given trip would take me only a few hours, and then end up getting home seven or eight hours later. But eventually the reality sunk in, and I began to plan for it.

On this first driving trip, the unexpected delays were all new to me, and so they did not seem that annoying yet. In fact, one of that day's unexpected delays was an exciting moment for me in the development of the project.

A Eureka Moment

When out on that first driving day, I was going to places which I had mapped out based on locations that I had already read about. I assumed at that point that this is what the project would consist of — going to and photographing locations which had been previously cataloged in books I had read.

But during that first drive, I had a moment which changed that assumption. While driving on Route 202 in Hunterdon County, traveling from one location to the next, I noticed a stone structure and sign on the side of the road, and pulled over to investigate. It turned out to be a monument to a military engagement which had occurred there in 1776, known as the Flemington Raid. This monument was *not* one of the historic sites that I had mapped out for the day, and had not previously seen any mention of it in the books and articles I had read.

This was a big moment for me. I had found something that I hadn't known would be there. Not only was this exciting and unexpected, but it also signified a change in the scope of the project on my very first day out.

As time went on, finding new locations became a major part of the project. Finding the unexpected was one of the things that would maintain my interest over the years of working on the project.

I hope that the people who now use the website as a guide to exploring New Jersey's Revolutionary War history will have similar experiences. I tried to be as thorough as possible in cataloging the state's Revolutionary War historic sites, and in the end included descriptions of 650 individual locations. But as extensive as the website's listings are, they are not a complete listing of every location in New Jersey associated with the Revolutionary War. So I hope that those who go out exploring the state based on my work have the same sense of excitement when they stumble on to something new that I had not listed, and get excited about the prospect of finding more.

CHAPTER 5

NEW JERSEY - WAR ZONE

When traveling around New Jersey today, it can be difficult to envision how life was for its citizens in the 1700's. It is harder still to envision that those citizens were living in a war zone. But from 1776 until 1783, the Revolutionary War was an ever-present fact of life for the citizens of New Jersey. Several important Revolutionary War battles, and many minor ones, occurred in the state. However, the effects on the population of living in a war zone went far beyond the actual battles.

There were soldiers in and around New Jersey for most of the war. At various times, American, British, Hessian, and French troops marched through, and encamped in the state. One of the most important ramifications of this was that these armies often needed food. For the farmers of New Jersey, this all-too-often meant that their food was confiscated by passing armies — food which might have represented an entire season's farm work. There was little that the farmers could do to stop their crops and livestock from being taken. If hundreds or thousands of armed men were hungry for the food on your farm, there was not much you could do to keep them from taking it.

During my research, I came across many sad stories of people losing not only their food, but also their property and possessions. Valuables were stolen. Fences were torn down for army firewood. Tools were confiscated for military use. To fully appreciate these losses, it is important to remember that possessions were much harder to replace in the 1700's than they are today.

We now live in a world where most items can be replaced quickly and easily, either in well-stocked stores with extensive inventories, or by ordering online, where overnight delivery is often an option. On top of this, credit is readily extended for people to purchase what they need without having to truly pay for it until much later. These factors create a convenience of availability in our culture which we often take for granted.

This convenience of availability did not exist for the people who lived at the time of the Revolutionary War, and so the loss of important items would be particularly hard on them. To illustrate this point, let us look at the example of Garrett Durie, a farmer and blacksmith who lived in Bergen County at the time of the Revolutionary War. At different times, Durie's farm was raided by British and by American troops who took food from him. On one occasion, not only his food, but also much of his blacksmithing tools and equipment were taken from him by British troops. This meant that he was being deprived of his ability to work as a blacksmith, until he could either make or acquire new tools, which could have been a difficult and lengthy process. It was the 1700's — there was no local Home Depot or Lowes where Durie could buy new tools.

Such hardships caused by the movements of troops across the state could be intensified by the fact that there may have been little warning that they were coming. Information did not travel as quickly then as it does now. Today, events that happen on the other side of the planet are broadcast live here on televisions, computers, and phones. Twenty-four-hour news stations and the Internet have helped to create a world of immediate information that would have truly amazed our ancestors. In the Revolutionary War era, none of the technology existed that now spreads information so quickly. Even the telegraph and the telephone would not be invented until almost a century later. Therefore, it would often take some time before people learned of events which occurred only a few miles away. As a result, there were occasions when a town or village had no forewarning that thousands of soldiers were marching in their direction.

A dramatic example of this occurred in January 1777. After winning important victories at Trenton and Princeton, General George Washington made a last-minute decision to take the American Army — known as the Continental Army — to Morristown for winter quarters. (At that time, armies usually did not fight in the winter, and would make camp at a given location until the springtime.)

When Washington and his army of approximately three-thousand men marched into Morristown which was then a village of only about two hundred and fifty people, the villagers were taken completely by surprise. The soldiers had to be fed, sheltered, and kept warm for the winter, and the residents of Morristown had to simply adjust to this new reality without any warning.

Morristown is a much more populated and built-up place today, but the center of the town is still an area known as the Morristown Green. It has been the heart of Morristown for centuries. You can visit the Morristown Green today, and try to picture the scene of the Continental Army arriving unexpectedly, back in that time when New Jersey was a war zone.

CHAPTER 6

EXPLORING THE STATE

The *Revolutionary War New Jersey* website project involved many different facets: researching, looking for information, making phone calls, visiting libraries, writing. But what was usually the most exciting part of the project was discovering and exploring the New Jersey locations where the history actually occurred.

My hope with creating the website was that it would inspire people to get out and explore for themselves — to feel their own sense of discovery. I have that same hope in writing this book.

Reading about history and watching historical documentaries are enjoyable and rewarding experiences. But nothing quite matches the feeling of actually standing in the locations where the history occurred. Visiting a home where George

Washington, Alexander Hamilton, or Benjamin Franklin stayed gives you a direct and tactile connection to those people who so profoundly shaped our history.

I believe that one of the best ways to get someone interested in history is to show them historic places right in their own neighborhood. One of the greatest joys I have received from the project is when someone tells me that they read about a location on the website that they had previously driven by a hundred times without knowing what it was.

I always want people to truly make the connection that the events described on the website took place *here* in their own state. I hope that upon learning about this local history, people acquire some feeling of possession of that history, and understand that it is part of their heritage as citizens. I realize that not everyone will take the next step from that feeling and become full-fledged history buffs, and that is OK. I believe that simply investing people with a connection to the history around them can bring about a historical understanding which benefits our society.

Houses of History

I visited many historic houses during the project. Some were used by General George Washington as a headquarters, others were simply the houses of ordinary citizens who lived there during the war. All of these houses have their own story to tell.

One thing that I always take note of in a historic house is the sunlight coming in through the windows. This is of particular interest to me because it is one thing that will not have changed in the past two centuries. If you are standing in a room where Alexander Hamilton was, and it is mid-day in winter, the angle of the sunlight coming through the windows will be the same for you as it would have been at mid-day in winter for him. Many things have changed dramatically since the Revolutionary War era, but the relative position of the sun and earth remain the same.

The angle of the sunlight may seem an insignificant thing to some, but it always mattered to me. Of course, if you begin your own journey of exploration through historic houses, the sunlight through the windows may not interest you much. The important thing is that you will find the little details which are of particular interest *to you*.

Some of the state's Revolutionary War houses are privately owned, and are not open to the public. In these cases, we can only enjoy viewing them from the outside. While I sometimes experienced disappointment at not being able to see the inside of these houses, in another way it made me happy that life continues to go on in them. That families still make their homes in structures that people have lived in since the 1700's. It gives a sense of continuity of the community.

Walking the Cemeteries

One of the unusual aspects of the project was how much time I spent in cemeteries. In many cases, I spent hours in old cemeteries walking up and down the rows of graves, looking for those marked as Revolutionary War soldiers.

In some cases, extensive historical records exist for a given cemetery, or a modern researcher has compiled detailed information. But often, no such records exist, and so walking around the cemetery was the only way to discover who was buried there.

One thing that took me a while to remember and plan for, was that cemeteries are mainly grass, so if you walk around a cemetery in the morning, you will likely be walking across grass which is wet with dew. Do yourself a favor if you pick a day to go out cemetery exploring: take an extra pair of socks and sneakers to change into, or wear boots, so that you don't have to spend the rest of your day exploring in wet feet, as I often did. (This may be the most useful information that you get from this book!)

I discovered many of the cemeteries listed on the website by accident, as I drove around looking for something else. If I saw what looked like an old cemetery, I'd get out of the car and explore it. Many of these discoveries happened when I was lost, an all-too-common occurrence for me.

Lost Again

If I have a super power, it is the ability to get lost anywhere, at anytime. I have a very limited sense of direction, and often get confused as to which way I am going, even when I am driving in an area I have been in many times.

I took my first trips for the project using only printouts of Google Maps directions. A few months later, I got a GPS device. For the remainder of the project, I used a combination of both Google Maps printouts and the GPS. But somehow I still got lost on many occasions!

This was especially true in some of the more rural areas of the state, where Google Maps can be inaccurate about small dirt roads, and where GPS would sometimes get confused.

Getting lost could be the source of great frustration, especially on a day when I had already been driving around for many hours but it did have its own rewards. It was often while lost that I would discover some location that I had not been looking for, and in fact had not known previously that it existed.

So my advice to you when you go out to do your own exploring is, don't worry too much about getting lost, or getting on the wrong road. You may discover something even more interesting than what you were originally looking for, and it may be something that many people aren't aware of.

Give Yourself the Gift of Exploring

As I stated before, exploring the actual historic sites was one of the things that kept me interested through the seven-and-a-half years of the project. I do admit that there were periods during the long project when that feeling of excitement about the exploration started to fade in me, and it began to feel routine. But that never lasted too long; some new location would be particularly interesting, and the thrill of exploration would come back to me.

That excitement of exploring history first-hand in the places it occurred is a wonderful feeling. Go out and experience it for yourself.

CHAPTER 7

MY FAVORITE TOWN

During the seven-and-a-half years of the project, I had the privilege of visiting, researching, and photographing over 200 towns and cities in New Jersey. Small towns. Large towns. Rural. Suburban. Cities. Each place had its own feel, and I enjoyed visiting most of them. When I look at a map of New Jersey now, I have tactile memories associated with so many of the town names I see.

Not only did each town have its own feel, but each visit was its own experience, with its own circumstances. Often, my positive or negative recollections of a town are influenced by such factors as what the weather was like when I was there, if I got lost, or if I got stuck in traffic.

I am often asked what was my favorite town that I visited. I always have the same answer — Cranbury.

Cranbury is a town in Central Jersey's Middlesex County that has a historic feel. Many of the houses are old, and I remember being impressed that some of the houses had year plaques on them to specify when they had been built — this was a town that cared about its history!

I visited Cranbury about a year into the project. It was early November 2010. I arrived there shortly after sunrise — my favorite time of day. It was sunny and a little chilly — my favorite type of weather. It was, in short, a perfect autumn morning for me.

I was in Cranbury to photograph a couple of locations associated with George Washington, Alexander Hamilton, and the Continental Army having been there prior to the Battle of Monmouth in 1778. There is also a historic cemetery where many Revolutionary War veterans are buried. I also discovered a couple of other Revolutionary War sites that I had not known about prior to getting there. All of these locations are along a mile stretch of Main Street, which meant that I could simply park my car, and then walk to all the places. I love walking, and I hate driving, so this was the perfect type of location for me to explore. Because it was early, very few people were out, and for the most part, I had the street to myself.

I can vividly remember standing in a small field that contains a marker commemorating the encampment of the Continental Army. Alongside the field ran Cranbury Brook, and across the road overlooks Brainerd Lake. I can feel how the sun felt, and how dazzling the sunlight looked reflecting off the lake. Everything just felt right.

I took many other trips throughout New Jersey during the project. Some were unenjoyable, some were routine, and others were wonderful. But I never again had a moment when everything felt so right as that crisp, sunny, autumn morning in Cranbury, walking alone up and down Main Street.

I have never been back to Cranbury, and most likely I never will. The vision I have of that morning is so perfect, that I would rather leave it as it is. I am sure that Cranbury is a wonderful place at any time, but I know that I could never quite recapture the feeling that I had that morning.

However, I do recommend that if you find yourself in Middlesex County, and would like to make a stop in a nice town with a historic feel, visit Cranbury, and take a walk down Main Street. I'll be there in spirit.

CHAPTER 8

CARS

I'm not a car guy. I don't particularly enjoy driving. I have no mechanical aptitude for maintaining or fixing cars. I have never had a desire to own a fancy or impressive car. But long drives to locations all over New Jersey were a big part of the project, so it was essential to have a reliable vehicle.

When I began the *Revolutionary War New Jersey* project in 2009, I was driving a car that was already twenty-one years old — a 1988 Buick Century. The outside of the car looked terrible, and my friends regularly made fun of it. However, it was a fairly reliable car that still drove reasonably well. Besides, I really didn't have the money to get anything better.

Fortunately, I had a major asset to help keep the car, and therefore the project, going — my mechanic Paul. (Note that this is a different Paul than the one mentioned in Chapter 1.) I would often stop by Paul's service station before I had to make a particularly long drive, and he would check over the basics of my car — fluids, oil, tires, etc. — and wouldn't charge me for his time. When my car did need fixing, he would always make the repairs at a reasonable price, and was understanding about extending me credit until I was able to pay him. He was interested in, and encouraging about, my project. Given the large amount of long driving trips the project required, having a friendly, trustworthy, and dependable mechanic like Paul was invaluable.

But even with Paul's help, my 1988 Buick could not endure the driving demands of the project indefinitely. In March 2011, I was having some trouble with the car, and brought it to Paul to look it over. He told me that this time the car was beyond fixing.

So on March 11, 2011, I said goodbye to the Buick. I wanted to pay a (hopefully) amusing tribute to the car, and so I wrote and sent the following email to my friends that day:

> "Dear friends,
>
> "Over the past year and a half, I have driven thousands of miles to every corner of New Jersey, while working on my *Revolutionary War New Jersey* website project. I have traveled to every part of the state — finding, cataloging, and photographing all of the Revolutionary War historic sites in New Jersey.
>
> "Throughout the thousands of driving miles, my constant and faithful companion has been my trusty 1988 Buick Century. It endured many all-day

drives to all corners of New Jersey, many on bad NJ roads, which in some rural parts of the state aren't even paved.

"But alas, the *Revolutionary War New Jersey* project took its toll on the old Buick, and today it breathed its last.

"Over the years, my Buick Century has been the target of many jokes from many people who laughed at its looks.

"It wasn't much to look at, I will grant the scoffers.

"However, for the $600 I paid for it in 2005, it never let me down. Under a different set of driving conditions, I believe my trusty Buick Century could have made it several more years. But the Revolutionary War project just proved too much for this old and weary automobile.

"My trusty Buick Century has died in the service of the Revolutionary War cause, nearly 230 years after the war ended.

"So, give a moment of silent reflection tonight for my now departed 1988 Buick Century — the last casualty of the Revolutionary War.

"AL"

Fortunately, when I retired the Buick, Paul had a good used car at his garage that he was able to sell me for $800. It was a 1994 Oldsmobile that had previously belonged to his mother. His mother had not driven the car very much, and so even though the car was seventeen years old, it only had eighty-four thousand miles on it. And Paul had maintained the car for her while she owned it, so it had always been taken care of by a good mechanic.

And so, I was back on the road. The Oldsmobile would last me until the end of the project six years later. And although it needed occasional repairs, it only broke down on me one time during all of the many long Revolutionary War drives I was to take over those years.

The Oldsmobile did have one major drawback — the air conditioner did not work. The lack of air conditioning was made worse by the fact that the passenger-side window could not be rolled down to get more of a breeze in. This made any drives I took on hot summer days extremely unpleasant!

CHAPTER 9

PULASKI STATUE

General Casimir Pulaski was a Polish officer who came to America to fight on the American side in the Revolutionary War. He was a supporter of the cause of American Independence, and had strong beliefs about freedom.

Pulaski is an early example of the United States as a concept based on a set of ideals which were open to anyone who came here, from wherever they came from — a nation of immigrants. As a country, we have not always lived up to those ideals, but those ideals represent us at our best.

Pulaski is surprisingly well-represented in New Jersey today. There are four statues of Pulaski in New Jersey, more than any Revolutionary War figure other than George Washington. The four Pulaski statues are located in Garfield, Paterson, Pennsauken, and Wallington. The Pulaski Skyway is also named in his honor.

****

In the summer of 2011, I was in Wallington to photograph the statue of Pulaski there. It was a bright, sunny day, the best kind of day for photographing outside. The statue is about ten feet tall, so I had brought a ladder with me to photograph it from a higher vantage point.

While I was photographing the statue, an elderly gentleman walking by stopped, looked at me taking the photos, and in a very heavy accent asked me, "Are you Polish?"

I replied, "Yes," by which I meant that I am of 50% Polish descent. (On my Mom's side, my ancestry is all Polish.)

However, he took my answer to mean that I was from Poland, or could at least speak the language, so he proceeded to talk very excitedly to me in Polish. Unfortunately, I can't speak a word of Polish, so I could not understand him. I was able to convey to him in gestures that I could not understand Polish. As it turned out, he could not speak any English beyond asking me if I were Polish, so we could not further communicate. We smiled and shook hands, and he was off.

At first, I was disappointed that we had been unable to communicate. I would have liked to have learned more about him, and hear what his knowledge and thoughts about Pulaski were.

After that initial disappointment passed, I began to look at the experience in a different light. It made me realize how these public commemorations of our history can help people connect with that history. In this Polish gentleman's case, I did not know how long he had been in the United States, and I could not know if he had much knowledge of American history. But

I did know that having this statue of Pulaski in his neighborhood was a source of pride to him as a man from Poland.

I encountered and spoke with hundreds of people during my seven-and-a-half years of work on the project — librarians, archivists, historic site docents, and others. And yet, this man who I met only briefly, and with whom I had been unable to communicate, is one of the people who stands out most in my memory, because of the pride he showed in that statue, and the potential I see in that pride.

In his case, the connection to that Pulaski statue, and the history it represented, was based on his being Polish. And every other person has their own potential connection to interest them in history, based on their own background, passions, and experiences. The more we publicly celebrate and represent our local history, the more likely that each individual can find the particular connection that might interest them in history. They may not take the next step of becoming a total history buff, but if they can at least make a connection to history, I believe that it can benefit them and our society.

CHAPTER 10

THE HISTORY CONNECTION

It always makes me sad when I hear someone say, "I hate history," or "History is so boring." I try to tell them that what they really mean is that it was presented to them in a boring way when they were young, and that made them think they hate it.

When history is reduced to making students memorize dates and dry facts for a test, it takes all the drama and excitement out of it. (Many students forget those dates the day after the test anyway.) But when history focuses on the *stories* of those who have lived before us it is much more likely to interest someone. Everyone likes a good story — that is why people read novels, and watch movies and television shows. It is also why people who are known to be good storytellers tend to be popular in social settings. Human beings simply can't resist a good story.

Therefore, if a person does not do well with learning dates, it is best to start by helping them understand the stories of history. Those stories of what people did, and the consequences of those actions, help to convey the concepts and ideas of history, which are what really matter. If someone can understand the ideas and importance of a given historic era, but gets confused about the exact dates when things occurred, that is okay. The important thing is to have developed an overview of the time period, and its place in the overall human story. They can always look up the dates when they need to.

There is of course nothing wrong with knowing the dates of historic events. I, for example, like to know the dates, because it helps me put things in perspective better if I understand the exact chronology of events. But not everyone thinks that way.

Many people enjoy history in some form without ever thinking of it as history. Often people who say that they don't like history because it was their most boring subject at school can tell you many things about the background story of their favorite sports teams, musical acts, or movie stars. Whether or not the person realizes it, those things are all part of history. Because history is everything that has ever happened. And every thing has its own history. The lives we are living today will be part of history tomorrow. Once a person makes these connections, they can develop an interest in — and even a passion for — history.

I first identified myself as someone who was "into history" in my early twenties. At that time, I started reading books about American history, and I was hooked. But in reality, I had been interested in history my whole life; I had just never thought of it that way.

When I was nine years old, I discovered the thing that remains my favorite topic all these years later — the Beatles. By the time I became seriously interested in them, they had been broken up for seven years, so I did not experience their story in real time. But I was so captivated by their music that I wanted to know everything I could about them.

I began by reading any books about the Beatles that I could get my hands on. I then took it deeper, and wanted to know more about their time period. I started to learn about the events of the 1960's which had swirled around them, but which I had not been alive to witness. I began to explore the music of 1950's Rock 'n' Roll, which had inspired them to become musicians. I even began reading the 1800's authors Lewis Carroll and Edgar Allan Poe, simply because they had appeared on the famous cover of the Beatles' *Sgt. Pepper's Lonely Hearts Club Band* album.

All the while I was learning about history on my own initiative. However, I never really connected it with the history I was being taught in school. I did like history in school a bit, even when it was presented in a boring fashion, but nothing sparked my interest enough to make me want to pursue it further. Looking back, I can see that there were many ways to connect the dots from what I was being taught in school to what I was reading on my own, but those connections were never shown to me. I had to discover them for myself years later as a young adult.

My own story is not particularly important; I use it only as an example. Many other children had their own interests which could have been used to help them connect to history. That potential still exists for those history-averse children who are now adults. It is just a matter of helping them to make their own history connection.

While it gives me great pleasure to hear a history buff tell me that they enjoy the *Revolutionary War New Jersey* website, one of the best compliments I can receive is when someone who was not previously into history tells me that they found something on the website interesting. My hope is that by having found something to spark their interest, they can go on to realize that they *do* like history. And not just Revolutionary War history, but all kinds of history.

It is important to have a society that is connected to its past. When we knew the history of our country — the good and the bad — it helps us to better understand our own time, and hopefully make better-informed choices for the future.

CHAPTER 11

THE HARD WINTER

Our experiences of winters in the modern world is much different than those who lived in earlier times. We live and work in buildings with central heating. We have hot water coming out of our faucets. We have supermarkets stocked with all kinds of food in the winter, including fresh fruit and vegetables flown in from warmer climates where they are grown.

After a snow storm, we have snow plows which come out and clear our roads, which we can then drive on inside of comfortable, heated cars that take us quickly to our destination. We do not have to walk miles through deep snow to get where we are going, as people once did.

Most aspects of life were harder for those living in the 1700's, but winters were in many ways the worst time of the year, when all the day-to-day struggles of their already hard lives were exacerbated. This was often particularly true for soldiers.

The Troops in Winter.

Writing about a war involves spending much time research-ing and thinking about tragic events and circumstances. This was certainly true of the years I spent working on the *Revolutionary War New Jersey* project.

Accounts of soldiers killed, wounded, and maimed in battle are obvious examples of the sad stories one encounters. Less obvious — but just as sad in their own way — are some of the stories of what soldiers experienced when they weren't fighting, especially in the winter months.

In earlier times like the 1700's, armies tended not to fight during the winter. Instead, they would have to find a place to encamp for the season, where hundreds or thousands of soldiers would need to find food and shelter in the difficult winter circumstances of the time.

The most famous story of winter hardship for American soldiers during the Revolutionary War is the winter of 1777-1778 that they spent at Valley Forge, Pennsylvania. Every school child hears the story of Valley Forge, and even Americans who can't recall the details will at least associate the name Valley Forge with winter army hardships.

But while Valley Forge may be the most famous winter, it was not actually the worst winter for American soldiers during the war. That distinction belongs to a place in New Jersey — Morristown.

Morristown

General George Washington and the American Army — known as the Continental Army — first encamped in Morristown early in the war, during the winter of 1777.

They returned to Morristown several years later, for the winter of 1779-1780. While Washington and his staff made their headquarters at Ford Mansion (which still stands in Morristown), ten to twelve thousand American soldiers encamped several miles away in a wooded area known as Jockey Hollow. The conditions they were to suffer through that winter were beyond anything they could have anticipated.

The winter was a brutal one. The soldiers experienced great hardship, hunger and cold. Twenty-eight separate snow storms are recorded to have fallen that winter. It was so continuously cold that for the first time in recorded history, the waters around New York City froze over, and were closed to shipping for weeks at a time.

In the midst of these extreme weather conditions, the soldiers had to cut down trees and build their own huts. And throughout, there was a serious shortage of food.

Joseph Plumb Martin, who was a soldier encamped at Jockey Hollow that winter, later wrote this harrowing account of what he and his fellow soldiers experienced during their winter encampment there:

> "The winter of 1779 and '80 was very severe; it
> has been denominated 'the hard winter,' and hard it
> was to the army in particular, in more respects than
> one. The period of the Revolution has repeatedly

been styled 'the times that tried men's souls.' I often found that those times not only tried men's souls, but their bodies too; I know they did mine, and that effectually...

"At one time it snowed the greater part of four days successively, and there fell nearly as many feet deep of snow, and here was the keystone of the arch of starvation. We were absolutely, literally starved. I do solemnly declare that I did not put a single morsel of victuals into my mouth for four days and as many nights, except a little black birch bark which I gnawed off a stick of wood, if that can be called victuals. I saw several of the men roast their old shoes and eat them, and I was afterwards informed by one of the officers' waiters, that some of the officers killed and ate a favorite little dog that belonged to one of them. If this was not 'suffering' I request to be informed what can pass under that name. If 'suffering' like this did not 'try men's souls,' I confess that I do not know what could."

CHAPTER 12

A SENSE OF PLACE

When I began the project, my intention was to learn and understand as much as I could about what my home state had been like at the time of the Revolutionary War. I wanted to learn how New Jersey looked then, how it functioned, what buildings were here, and — most importantly — what the people were like.

I feel a real connection to the people who lived before me that called New Jersey home. They walked over the same hills and flats I do, passed by the same rivers and lakes, looked out on the same Atlantic Ocean from the same shore, and experienced New Jersey weather and seasons much like I do. I have no blood relation to most of them, but the sense of shared places makes me *feel* related to them. That feeling makes me want to better understand what they experienced.

Over the course of seven-and-a-half years, I did get to learn a great deal about New Jersey and its citizens in the 1700's.

But something else occurred which I hadn't really considered at the start - I got to learn more about my state as it is now in the 21st Century. And I learned about it and experienced it in ways that I most likely never would have otherwise.

All of the time I spent driving and walking around the state to figure out what occurred in the Revolutionary War era, also meant that I was seeing the state as it is now. And seeing *all* of it — the suburbs, the cities, the rural areas, the farmlands, the shore. The times I spent in all of these areas was extensive; I wasn't just "passing through." I walked around streets, church-yards, cemeteries and parks. I spent time in government build-ings and libraries in all parts of the state, and experienced how they looked and felt different in different areas. I stopped in stores and got to talk to people all over the state.

Different parts of the state have their own personalities, and I feel that I have gotten to understand them all a bit.

During the years of work on the project, most of my thoughts and energy were focused on New Jersey. I was only out of the state for a few brief times during those seven-and-a-half years, and most of those times were part of my research. (For example, while researching the site of Washing-ton's Crossing of the Delaware River, I spent a little time on the Pennsylvania side of the river as part of the research.) Other than those times, I only left New Jersey on two occasions — both on day trips to New York City.

I realize that if I had not spent so many years researching in New Jersey, I could have spent time exploring more far-off places in other parts of the country and the world. The amount of my life spent on the project means that in the end I will have explored less of the world than I could have otherwise. This could make it seem like the project limited my horizons, but I choose to look at it from another point of view - that I had the privilege to explore and experience my home state in a way that most people will never get to. I may not get to visit all fifty states of the country in this lifetime, but I have gotten to thoroughly explore all twenty-one counties of the state I call home.

CHAPTER 13

THE HELICOPTER INCIDENT

Most of the many driving trips I took for the project were single-day affairs. But on several occasions, I mapped out a larger plan, and stayed overnight or longer in a hotel in whatever area of the state I was researching at the time.

On one such trip in summer 2011, I was returning to my hotel after a long day of driving and photographing for the project. It had been a good and productive day, but I was feeling tired from having driven over seven hours. Also, it had been a hot summer day, and I had endured it in my car with no air conditioning. I was looking forward to getting back to my air-conditioned hotel room and relaxing.

The hotel I was staying at was located on a highway. The entrance to the hotel parking lot was a small turnoff from the highway's shoulder that did not give drivers much advance notice it was coming. Unfortunately, I did not notice the hotel entrance until a second too late, and so, I drove past it. I was slightly annoyed by this, but figured it was not a big deal; I would just turn off at the next highway exit, and then double-back around to the hotel.

What I didn't realize was how long it would take me to get back to the hotel. I had to make a U-turn at the next exit, and then drive on the other side of the highway until I could make another U-turn to get me back on the correct side of the highway, where I would have to drive another mile to get back to the hotel. Not the end of the world – but also not what I felt like doing after spending hours driving in my hot car.

When I did make it back to the hotel about ten minutes later, I missed the entrance *again*. Now I was really annoyed. Not only had I stupidly missed the hotel entrance a second time, but this time I knew up front how much I would have to drive to get back again.

So I went through the whole turn-around-and-come-back-again process a second time. Once again: several miles, two U-turns, ten minutes.

Incredibly, after all that, I managed to miss the hotel entrance a *third* time! But this time I refused to drive all the way around again. I pulled onto the shoulder lane, and realized that if I were to back up on the highway shoulder about 200 feet, I could reach the hotel entrance that way.

I don't advocate anyone making a reckless move like backing up 200 feet on a highway shoulder while cars are speeding by on the highway. But at that moment I thought, "The hell with it. I'd rather take the risk than have to drive all the way around again."

When I had gone about fifty feet in reverse, I suddenly heard a police siren go on. I turned my head and saw that a police car driving directly across from me on the other side of the highway had turned his siren on and was taking off really fast, just after I had started my ill-advised highway shoulder backup.

"Oh no!," I thought. "He saw what I'm doing, and now he's coming after me!"

I figured that I had a minute or so before the police car could get around to my side of the highway and into the hotel parking lot. So I continued backing up on the shoulder, got to the hotel entrance, and pulled into the parking lot behind the hotel and parked my car. I turned off the ignition and thought, "Let me just get out of the car and into the hotel right away, and I'm safe."

However, right at that moment, I heard the police siren approaching and then saw the police car pull into the hotel parking lot and park about 50 feet to my rear left. I looked away, and didn't want to look back in his direction, so as to not look suspicious.

I decided that I would just wait in the car until he came over, and then try to nicely convince him to not give me a ticket.

So I sat in the car waiting, but the officer did not come over. I started to get paranoid.

I should point out that while I have a generally happy and optimistic outlook, I do have a paranoid streak. And when that paranoid streak kicks in, it starts to intensify quickly. And this was definitely a circumstance for paranoia.

"The policeman is trying to mess with my head!," I thought. "He's putting psychological pressure on me by making me wait and worry!"

As I sat and waited, I got more and more paranoid. It was about to get worse.

I heard a sound coming from overhead. I looked up through my windshield and saw what was making the noise — there was a police helicopter hovering!

Now I was *really* flipping out. The police were going to an incredible amount of trouble to put psychological pressure on me. They had actually called out a police helicopter!

A bunch of thoughts raced through my head: "Maybe backing up on a highway shoulder is a much bigger offense than I would have imagined." "Maybe they take highway traffic violators *very* seriously around here." "Maybe if they went to all this trouble, they are actually going to arrest me instead of just giving me a ticket."

I'm not sure how long I sat in the car waiting. It felt like hours, but it was probably more like a few minutes.

Finally, I just couldn't take it anymore. I was going to get out of the car and start walking towards the hotel. Let them stop me and arrest me, but at least the waiting would be over.

As I got out of my car, I could hear the helicopter hovering overhead. I could see the reflections of the police car's flashing lights (although the sirens had been turned off.) I was trying to act casual, but was failing miserably.

I started walking towards the hotel, but no policeman approached me. Damn, they were really taking this psychological pressure thing all the way! I felt like I was about to crack. I was ready to throw up my hands and shout, "I can't take this anymore! Just arrest me and get it over with!"

But instead, I finally decided to turn and look directly at the police car. From where I now was, I had a clear view. I could see that the policeman had gotten out of his car, and was questioning someone in a dilapidated vehicle parked in the back of the parking lot. He paid no attention to me.

I suddenly realized that the police car and helicopter had absolutely nothing to do with me. It had all been a coincidence. Whatever they were investigating just happened to occur at the same time I was backing up on the highway, and just happened to involve someone who was in that hotel parking lot. I made it back into my hotel room, and collapsed on the bed.

CHAPTER 14

A MORE DISTANT PAST

The Revolutionary War era can seem like a long time ago. The war ended in 1783, which is 235 years ago as I write this. The technology and society of the 1700's was quite different than ours, making that time period feel even more distant.

During the course of the project, I spent a lot of time looking at and exploring buildings, churches, cemeteries, and houses that dated from the Revolutionary War era, and I was always intrigued by the fact that they were over two centuries old.

But in reality, 235 years is not very long in the scope of human history. It is only three lifetimes. Humans have lived on the earth for over three hundred thousand years, and recorded history dates back for five thousand.

Even the three hundred thousand years that humans have existed seems small when compared to the age of the earth, which scientists estimate to be four-and-a-half *billion* years. Throughout those billions of years, geological activity was shaping the land masses and terrain of the planet.

One of the most fascinating aspects of the project for me was realizing that some of the Revolutionary War sites I was exploring had ties to geological activity which occurred thousands and even millions of years ago. One of my favorite examples of this was the site of a summertime picnic of Revolutionary War officers.

On July 10, 1778, while traveling across North Jersey, General George Washington and some of his officers stopped by an impressive waterfall. One of the officers present, James McHenry, wrote the following description of the experience:

"In our route to Paramus, where part of the army had encamped in order to rest and refresh, we visited the falls of Pasaic. We crossed the river at an old bridge in very bad repair and in half a mile reached the falls.

"The rock to which they owe their birth is of considerable compass (covered in general with herbage, some trees and shrubbery). But besides the chasm into which the water throws itself there are several other fissures and deep dismemberments, formed as it would seem by nature in some of her violent operations. The falls tho' curious in themselves derive additional beauties from those objects with which they are connected...

" [The] conflict and the dashing of the water against the asperities and contrasted sides of the rock produces a fine spray that issuing from the cleft appears at a distance like a thin body of smoke. Near the bottom of the falls it exhibits a beautiful rainbow in miniature...

"A little above the falls the water glides over some ledges of rock of about 3 or 4 feet perpendicular in a very pretty manner...

"After viewing these falls we seated ourselves round the General under a large spreading oak within view of the spray and in hearing of the noise.

"A fine cool spring bub[b]led out most charmingly from the bottom of the tree. The travelling canteens were immediately emptied and a modest repast spread before us, of cold ham, tongue and some biscuit. With the assistance of a little spirit we composed some excellent grog. Then we chatted away a very cheerful half hour — and then took our leave of the friendly oak — its refreshing spring — and the meek falls of Pasaic less noisy and boisterous than those of Niagara, or the more gentle Cohoes or the waters of the Mohawk."

The place they were at, which McHenry calls "Pasaic Falls," is a seventy-seven-foot waterfall on the Passaic River that is now the Paterson Great Falls National Park. I visited the site several times during the course of my research. It was possibly the most impressive place I visited for the project. The sheer power of the falling water is amazing. Visiting the falls at different times is interesting because of the variations in the amount and power of the water based on how much rainfall there had recently been.

To me, the most delightful aspect of the falls is the rainbow effect mentioned by McHenry. If you are standing atop the falls at just the right times on a sunny day, you can see small rainbows forming in the spray coming off the falling water. Rainbows are one of my favorite things in the world, and I love the thought that Washington and his officers experienced them in the same spot that I did. Exploring Revolutionary War historic sites always gives me a feeling of connecting with events that occurred almost two-and-a-half centuries ago. But what made the Paterson Great Falls so much more interesting was that these waterfalls had existed long before Washington and his officers picnicked there. The water had been falling over these rock formations for approximately thirteen thousand years. But the rock formations themselves date back two-hundred *million* years, to when the Watchung Mountains were formed.

The Watchung Mountains stretch for forty miles from Central Jersey to North Jersey, through Somerset, Morris, Essex, Passaic, and Bergen Counties.

When people travel across New Jersey today, they generally take little notice of the Watchung Mountains, because modern roads and construction have created easy passways around, over, and through them. But at the time of the Revolutionary War era, they were still a reality that had to be taken into account when moving around New Jersey. The cliff walls of the Watchungs created obstructions for local citizens who sometimes had to travel miles out of their way to go around them to get where they were going.

The same cliff walls provided General George Washington and his troops with a strategic asset. It is important to remember that British forces occupied New York City for almost the entire war. This meant that they were always within striking distance of North and Central Jersey. Because of this, Washington regularly chose positions for his army behind the Watchungs, which allowed the cliff walls to serve as a protective barrier against British troops. This helped to offset the British superiority in manpower and military expertise.

The high vantage points on top of the Watchung Mountains also provided another benefit — they functioned as lookout sites to see over great distances if British troops were marching towards them from New York City. One can still get a sense of this today, as Watchung Mountain cliffs in places like Garrett Mountain Reservation and Washington Rock State Park provide some of the most dazzling views in New Jersey.

Throughout my research, I was continually reminded that one of the deciding factors in Washington's war strategy — and therefore one of the major reasons for New Jersey's importance in the Revolutionary War — was this series of mountains which were formed 200 million years before there even was a New Jersey, a George Washington, a British army, muskets or bullets. 200 million years even before Native Americans inhabited this area before the arrival of Europeans. 200 million years, in fact, before *any* human beings existed. Indeed, these mountains were actually formed at a time before some of the most famous dinosaurs, such as Tyrannosaurus Rex, existed.

Visiting Revolutionary War sites on the Watchung Mountains helps to put into perspective just how short a time period it has been since the Revolutionary War in the grand scheme of things. It can also give one a sense of awe to contemplate how short our own lives are, how short the life of the country has been, and even how short the length of all human history is, in relation to the age of the earth.

These locations are highlights of New Jersey. A trip to any of them provides three levels of enjoyment: their natural beauty, their connection to our Revolutionary War past, and their connection to a more distant past.

CHAPTER 15

THE PROJECT GROWS

What had started out as a relatively small project grew slowly but steadily over time. In fact, it took several years of work before I had a clear idea of its size and scope. The expansion happened in stages, but it is difficult to say exactly when those stages occurred. It can sometimes be hard to look back over the arc of your life and know precisely when things shifted. Sometimes there was a clear moment of demarcation, but more often things were affected from many different angles until one day you found yourself in a different place. In the case of *Revolutionary War New Jersey*, expansion occurred in several aspects of the project, one of which was the photos.

In an earlier chapter, I mentioned that starting with my first driving trip, I took up a great deal of extra time by shooting a lot of photos from every angle. I did this in the hope of getting good photos, to compensate for my lack of photography skills and experience. When I got home from my first trip, I realized the other half of this — that having taken so many photos meant a *lot* of extra time going through them, sorting them out, and deciding which ones to use.

My initial photos were taken with a Nikon Coolpix camera that I had borrowed from my Mom. Several months later, I bought my own Coolpix camera for $176.40; that camera would last me through the end of the project. I might have been better off with a more expensive camera, but the Coolpix served me well enough. Besides, I didn't want to have to learn any advanced settings on a better camera. My technological limitations definitely made me a "point and shoot" kind of guy.

Over time, I got a little better at taking photos, but I never came close to getting the quality of photos I would have liked. I realize that the website would look more impressive if it had been photographed by a team of professional photographers, but then it would not have been the same personal project. When I look over the completed website today, I know that I was the one standing at those historic sites taking the photos, and so I have the memories associated with taking them.

One simple but important tip for getting better photos did become apparent to me over time. Since almost all of the photos on the website were taken outside, the important thing was to learn to work with the position of the sun when taking photos. I began to understand that you want the sun facing the building, statue, or sign being photographed, not behind it. Therefore:

- If something faces East, shoot it in the morning.
- If it faces West, shoot it in the afternoon.
- If it faces South, you can get a good photo most times on a sunny day.
- If it faces North, the sun will always be behind it, so it is difficult to get a good photograph at any time of day.

After I had learned this lesson, I tried to plan my trips based on locations and times of day, by using Google Maps to determine in advance which direction things faced. This was not always possible, because sometimes I would be photographing things in the same area on the same day which happened to face different directions, so they couldn't face the sun at the same time of day.

Even though my photography skills improved slightly over time, I never got over the habit of shooting way too many photos, even though I constantly told myself I needed to stop wasting so much time by doing so.

By the time I reached 2013, I decided that the photos I had taken up until that time were not good enough, and I needed to go back to reshoot most of the photos I had already taken. This added a great deal of time to the project.

Another reason the project continued to expand was that I was regularly finding many more locations to include on the website than I had been aware of when I started. Originally, I had been working from lists I had in books, but over time I began to find more and more historic sites, either from additional reading, or from finding them while I was looking for something else. Either way, the amount of locations grew from 300 to 400 to 500 to 600 to 650. And each new location entry required its own driving, its own photography, its own research, and its own writing.

The biggest increase to the size and scope of the project came in the amount and depth of the research. At the beginning of the project, I had intended to accompany the photos with only brief text and basic information. But the longer I worked on the project, the more I wanted to include in-depth information. And the more I pursued in-depth information, the more critical I became in assessing facts. Ultimately, this led me to seeking out and researching the best sources of historical information, which are documents from the time period that the events occurred.

CHAPTER 16

GOING TO THE SOURCE

When I began work on the *Revolutionary War New Jersey* website, I had no real experience as a historian. I had spent a good portion of my life reading about a range of history topics, but I had not delved into the world of doing historic research with primary sources.

Primary sources are documents which were written at the time of the historic events you are researching, such as letters, journals, newspaper articles, and legal documents. These are in contrast with what are known as secondary sources, which are books and articles written by historians based on their own research.

I began work on the website by working mainly with secondary sources, but as time went on, I did more and more of my own research with primary sources. This was not a fully-planned change, nor did it happen all at once. It was more of a process that grew over time as I became more critical in assessing information.

Primary source research may seem intimidating or tedious at first. In some cases this can be true, particularly if you are working with dry documents like property deeds and legal paperwork. However, in the case of more personal documents, such as letters and journals, it can be a richly rewarding experience. It allows you to get as close as possible to the people of an earlier time, and to feel what they experienced.

Fortunately, a great deal of documentation exists from the Revolutionary War era. The population was largely literate, and a considerable amount of their letters and journals have survived, as well as newspapers and legal documents. This is a luxury in studying Revolutionary War era America that does not always exist when studying other earlier eras and societies.

Accessing and Assessing the Information

We live in a time of easy digital access to historic documents. For example, the National Archives' "Founders Online" database provides anyone interested in the Revolutionary War era with free access to thousands of transcribed letters and documents from that time period. This type of online archive allows the modern historian to conveniently access a wide range of documents which only decades ago would have required them to travel to libraries and archives all over the country to view them in person.

Of course, many old documents and books have not been digitized, and it is necessary to seek out physical copies. In these cases, public libraries and local historical societies are invaluable resources, because they often contain hidden gems of information. I am a bibliophile, and I always get more enjoyment reading a physical copy, but I certainly came to appreciate the easy accessibility of online documents. The important thing is that between the digital and physical, so much original documentation is available.

The value of these documents being accessible is that it makes it easier for you to verify information for yourself. If you are serious about learning about a historical topic, and read a book or website about it, check the author's source notes to see what documents they based their writing on. You can then seek out those documents to read them for yourself. You may find that you disagree with the author's understanding of the source documents. In some cases, there may be more than one equally valid interpretation of the source documents, and you may arrive at a different conclusion than the author.

All historians make errors. It is simply not humanly possible to do historic research and writing without getting some things wrong. Those of us who write about history make our best effort to be accurate, but even if one is as thorough as possible in researching a topic, one may simply misunderstand or misinterpret the sources they are working with.

In compiling the *Revolutionary War New Jersey* website, I made a great effort to work as much as possible from primary sources. I then put detailed source notes on the website so that readers can see where I obtained my information, read it for themselves, and assess the conclusions I drew.

Limitations

There are limitations to working with primary sources which should be kept in mind when writing history based on them. Just because a document dates from the time of an event, it does not necessarily mean that it is a completely accurate or truthful account.

Even if the document that you are reading was written the same day as the events it describes, the person writing it may have gotten some or all of the story wrong. They may have misunderstood what had occurred. They may have been poor at writing down information accurately. They may have been vain, and exaggerated their role in the events. Conversely, they may have been modest, and understated their role. Or they may have simply been lying.

Because, of these factors, one must always view the primary documents with a critical eye. It is always helpful to have more than one contemporaneous account of an event to compare and evaluate, but often you won't have that luxury.

However, even with the limitations that primary sources have, they are still the most valuable tool available to us to know about the thoughts and actions of the people who lived in earlier times.

Military and Political Correspondence

Reading the correspondence of military and political leaders of the Revolutionary War provides invaluable insight into the events of the war, and the decisions which led to those events. It is important to keep in mind that at that time there were no phone, Internet, or satellite technologies for people to talk with each other over distance. So if two people were communicating over distance, all of their communications were likely made by written letters. Therefore, if all of their letters to each other have survived, we can have a complete record of their communications.

Fortunately, an extensive amount of the written correspondence between the leading military and political figures of the era has survived. Most of the prominent people of that time were very thorough about saving their letters in an organized fashion. George Washington was particularly meticulous about keeping records of his correspondence.

I spent many hours reading military and political correspondence from the Revolutionary War era for the project. By far, the individual whose letters I read the most was George Washington, and he always kept my interest. Reading Washington's letters provides an insight into what he was thinking, feeling, and experiencing that you cannot get otherwise. Washington was the central figure of America for two decades, from his appointment as head of the Continental Army in 1775, until the end of his tenure as America's first president in 1797, so access to his correspondence is particularly valuable.

Letters and Journals of Ordinary Citizens

While reading the documents of the famous central characters of the time is interesting and educational, there is also great enjoyment and usefulness to be found in reading the letters and documents of ordinary citizens of the time. These documents give us insight into the views and experiences of ordinary citizens as great events occurred around them. Their perspectives are often very different from those who were in a position of authority.

The people of the Revolutionary War era wrote in a style that is somewhat different than ours. It may take a little time to acclimate yourself to their writing style, but I believe that you will find that it is well worth the effort. Beyond the educational value of reading their words, you may also find it to be enjoyable and enriching.

In the next chapter, we will take a look at the journals of two ordinary New Jersey residents during the Revolutionary War. One was a minister in Swedesboro, and the other was a young woman who lived in what is now West Orange.

CHAPTER 17

A SORROWFUL PAST

Much of what I researched and wrote about for the project was sad. That should not come as a surprise, because I was writing about a war. War is not just a bad thing, it is as bad as it gets. The necessity and justification for individual wars can be debated and evaluated, but what is not debatable is how awful the effects are — on the soldiers doing the fighting, and on the citizens whose lives are caught in the crossfire.

The soldiers in combat experienced something far beyond what most of the rest of us will ever have to. No amount of reading about war, watching war movies or documentaries, or even talking with veterans could ever make us truly feel what combat is like. When I wrote about battles, I would try to put myself in the soldiers' situation, and to imagine what it must have felt like knowing that a musket ball or bayonet might tear through you, or that you might have to watch the person next to you die in agony, or that you might have to kill an enemy soldier, but these things are simply beyond my experience. I could research the fighting, and do my best to describe it, but I could never actually feel the horror the soldiers felt.

I happened to be writing about the Revolutionary War, but I assume that anyone studying any war would have a similar experience. Depending on the war and the time period, the weapons would change, but the concept would remain. Whether it was the fear of a bayonet ripping through you in the Revolutionary War, or the dread of a gas warfare attack in World War I, the essential terror would remain. And those of us who are fortunate enough not to have lived through such things cannot truly grasp what they felt like. We can however, feel empathy for those who lived through it, even if they lived long before us.

The sadness I felt for the Revolutionary War soldiers extended far beyond their combat experiences. They regularly endured miserable conditions when they weren't fighting. They were far from their homes and families, often without sufficient food. They suffered through brutally cold winter encampments without proper clothing and shoes. The sadness I felt for those soldiers was sometimes overwhelming to me.

Civilians in the War Zone

The sadness I encountered and felt in researching the Revolutionary War was not just limited to the soldiers. There were also the effects that the war had on local citizens. They had their lives uprooted, and had their property destroyed or confiscated. And sometimes they experienced horrifying things.

It is important to understand how divided the population was during the Revolutionary War. Some people supported Independence, some remained loyal to the British, and others were somewhere in the middle. Often citizens on opposing sides turned on each other violently. Some of the saddest things I encountered were accounts of neighbors fighting with each other — destroying each other's property, and even killing each other — because they had chosen different sides. If there had been no split between the colonies and Britain to cause the Revolutionary War, these people would have most likely lived out their lives as friendly neighbors, visiting each other and going to each other's children's weddings. But because of the rifts caused by the war, these things were not to be.

In the course of my research, I spent much time reading the letters and journals of people who lived through these experiences. I was regularly filled with sadness, and sometimes horror. The story which disturbed me the most was one I found in the journal of a minister named Nicholas Collin.

Collin had emigrated from Sweden to America, where he became the minister of a church in Swedesboro in Central Jersey. He left behind a journal of his experiences which provides a vivid depiction of what it was like to live in the war zone as a non-combatant. In the spring of 1778, he wrote the following account in his journal of a horrific event he witnessed, involving the punishment inflicted by local citizens on a man who was caught conducting business with the British:

> "In the morning on Easter Day a terrific cry was heard near the church. When I came out I saw a terrible sight. A man, married to a woman of Swedish parents and in a way belonging to the congregation, was tied to a pine tree and was being whipped. He fainted at times, but when he recovered, the flogging continued both on [his] sides and back, so that the flesh was said to have been entirely crushed [and cut up]. Some days later he died. His crime was that he had profited by the forbidden trade."

A Sadder, Harder Time

The sadness of the Revolutionary War era goes beyond the war itself. To put it another way, even if there had been no war, life at that time would still have been filled with sadness and hardship. Living in 21st Century America, most of us live with a level of comfort and convenience that would have been inconceivable to people who lived in the 1700's. Things like air conditioning, central heating, refrigeration, modern mattresses and pillows, toilets and running water, far exceed the comforts that were available to even the wealthiest people alive in the 1700's.

They were living decades before the discovery of anesthesia, and so the dentistry and surgery of their time now look like barbaric tortures to us.

They also lived with a level of infant mortality that is chill-ing to contemplate. Deaths in childbirth, of both the child and mother, were commonplace. Many children who survived their birth did not live to adulthood. When you study that time period, you inevitably come across accounts of families who had many children, but none of them lived to adulthood. Faced with that reality, how did people live with what must have been a consistent and over-hanging sadness? It seems that they had to internalize that sadness, and accept that level of sorrow as something that was inevitable for them.

For a first-hand account of living in a time of high youth mortality, we can turn to the diary of Jemima Condict, a young woman who lived in an area called Pleasantdale in what is now West Orange, NJ. Jemima's diary contains not only her thoughts and anxieties about the Revolutionary War, but also gives a feeling of life — and death — in her small community. In one three-month period in 1776, she recorded over forty deaths of her neighbors, due to the "bloody flux" (dysentery) which caused people to waste away through continual bloody diarrhea. She identifies most of them as children.

Keep in mind that at the same time dysentery was ravaging Jemima's neighbors, they were also dealing with the realities of the war. Jemima expressed her despair, when she wrote in her diary, "What a time is this! A Sickly time & a very Dieing time & the People fleeing before there enemies."

Jemima married in 1779, and died later that year after giving birth to a son, Ira. She was only twenty-five years old. Her son Ira died at age twelve.

Jemima Conflict died almost two centuries before I was born. But reading her words is an example of how the experiences of those who came before us can still touch us, and fill us with sadness.

But what exactly is this sadness? When you think about it, it is an unusual and amazing capacity that human beings have — we can look back at people who are long gone and feel sad for them. We can feel compassion for people who lived centuries before us, even though we cannot help or console them. We cannot hope for them to have a better future, because their futures are over. Their stories have long since ended. But somehow we have the capacity to feel for them.

(Note that Jemima's spelling, grammar, and punctuation
have not been corrected or modernized.)

Year 1776 JULY 23, Did that Distressing Disorder the Blody flux Begin to rage in this Neighborhood. Rubin Harrison Lost his Son Adonijah the 29. he was the 2nd he had lost of that Name & AUGUST the 6th Then Died John Ogdens Child & was buried on the 8th Day.

AUGUST the 16th, Then Died Jered freman. he was taken Sick at newyork among the Sogers & was brought home & Died Soon After.

AUGUST. Isac freman also Lost two of his Children with the Same Distemper.

John freman Lost his Child AUGUST ye 17th

AUGUST ye 25 Died Sam smiths Child

AUGUST the 29th amos Burrel Lost his Child

the same month Sam Crane Lost one with fits

AUGUST the 30th then Died Timothy Crane With the Same Distemper

The same Day Died Joseph Peirsons Child

SEPTEMBER the 2nd Did Thomas fremans Daughter Dieh

SEPTEMBER ye 3rd Did John freman Depart this life

SEPTEMBER ye 4th Jonathan Smith Lost his Child

The Same Night Jonathan Condicts Dauter Died

SEPTEMBER ye 8th Did Jabez williams Child Die

Abel freman also has Lost one of his children & the widow of John freman has Lost one of hersh

John Dod lost one about the Same time

[Monday] the 9th then Died another of Jonathan Condicts Daughters Enock beach has Lost three of his Children in About a fortnight

Tuesday the 10th then Died Joseph williams wife. She has bin this many years Confind with the Remutsim.

71

Sunday SEPTEMBER the 15th then Departed this Life Grandfather harrison aged Ninety three years.

Tho he is old, age will not Save

Him nor others from the grave

Sunday ye 15 Day Died Jabes Regs & Sunday the 22 they Buried his third Child, two of them; a Son & Daughter was In their Prime cut of in the full Bloom of Youth; Tuesday the 24th then Died his Wife also. The Rest of the family is Left,

Tho of So many they are bereft.

Joseph freman also has Lost two of his Children With the Same Disorder. thaniel Taylor Lost one about ye same time Isac Smith Lost one of his Children

Jonathan tomkins Lost his wife the Same month With the Consumtion

SEPTEMBER the 21st then Died ruth williams Child

SEPTEMBER ye 27 Jeams Jones Lost his Child

SEPTEMBER ye 27 Died Thomas Stage

SEPTEMBER ye 28 Died moses Crane

SEPTEMBER ye 29 Departed this Life John Spear

OCTOBER the 4 Amos Dod Lost his Child

OCTOBER the 5th Amos tomkins Lost his Child

OCTOBER the 5th Then Died moses freman

OCTOBER the 9th then Died martha Harrison

Thomas Codamas has Lost one Child

Benjamin Boldwin Lost one of his Children

OCTOBER the 13 then Died elesabeth Crane

OCTOBER the 14 then Died elenor Boldwin

OCTOBER the 14 Did eli williams Child Die

OCTOBER the [*date uncertain*] Jonah ward Lost his Child

OCTOBER the 21 Died Sam wards Child & Soon after Lost another

OCTOBER ye 25 then Died amos harisons Child

The dear delights we hear injoy

& fondly Call our own

Are But fond Pleasures lent us now

To Be repaid a non

CHAPTER 18

STAY HUMBLE

The knowledge and understanding of the Revolutionary War that I acquired throughout the project was primarily focused on what occurred in New Jersey. I would be the first to acknowledge the limitations of my knowledge of the larger war. Anyone who specializes in other locations or other facets of the war would likely have a great deal to teach me about their areas of expertise.

Even within the framework of New Jersey, there were many different topics that I had to read about, ranging from military matters to farming to geological formations. Obviously, when looking into these many sub-topics, I could only take enough time to give myself a basic understanding of them, and then apply it to the larger story of the Revolutionary War in New Jersey.

My experiences were certainly not unique. Researching any wide-ranging historic subject would involve many smaller topics. Therefore, you have to continually make a choice of what sub-topics to study, and how thoroughly you study each of them. It is also true that you can never know before-hand which sub-topics would be the most important to your research. Something which you might think is not relevant to the topic you are researching might in fact be very important, but you might only discover its importance after you had studied it.

For example, if you were researching the politics or wars of a certain historic era, you might not take any time to study the fashions of that time period, because you assume that it is not relevant to what you are studying. However, it is possible that fashion may have actually had some important impact that you hadn't imagined. Perhaps the materials or dyes used in the clothing may have had economic and trade implications that affected politics or international relationships. Or perhaps not. That is the point — you really don't know what is important until after you have taken the time to research it.

Because of these factors, one should always stay humble about what one is researching. Always consider that, no matter how much you know, it is only a small part of the larger story, and that other people know things that you don't. Even when it comes to the things you know very well, it is good to be open to the possibility that you may be incorrect in your conclusions. It can keep you from finding a deeper truth if you are too confident in your assumptions.

The longer I worked on the project, the more I learned these lessons and tried to keep them in mind. I believe they were valuable lessons to learn, and I try to apply them to life as a whole, and not just historic research. I am nowhere near as successful in applying these lessons as I'd like to be, but it is something to strive for.

Studying the Revolutionary War provides us with the perfect example of someone who not only understood these concepts, but fully employed them to his benefit, and — more importantly — to the benefit of the country. That person was George Washington. His leadership style as a general, and later as our first president, shows that he truly understood the benefits of surrounding himself with people who were more knowledgeable about certain topics than he was.

He knew that he had his range of knowledge and understanding of certain topics, and felt comfortable seeking the information and opinions of others who knew things he didn't. Part of what made Washington such a true leader was having this humility.

Washington's acknowledging that he had things to learn from others was not a sign of weakness; it was rather a sign of his inner strength and self-confidence. This is a lesson worth learning by anyone in a position of power today.

CHAPTER 19

AN IMPERFECT PAST

Studying history allows us to observe the great triumphs and progress made over the course of human civilization. But it also forces us to look at the bad, cruel, and sometimes horrific things people have done.

While working on the project, I was certainly confronted with tales of cruel behavior and brutal events: The sufferings and tragic deaths of soldiers on the battlefield. Civilians who had their property confiscated or destroyed. Neighbors who turned against one another and committed senseless acts of violence on each other's families and homes. Court-martialed soldiers who were punished with whippings or executions. Prisoners of war kept in awful conditions.

I was often shaken by such stories. But as sad as these stories were, they really did not come as a surprise to me. I was, after all, writing about a war.

However, there was one sad reality I was confronted with that did come as a surprise to me — that slavery had existed in New Jersey to a much greater extent than I had previously known. I had, of course, known of slavery's role in the history of the country as a whole, but I had never really associated slavery with New Jersey. Over the course of the project, I came to learn otherwise.

Unexpected Discovery

My project was focused specifically on the Revolutionary War events which occurred in New Jersey. Slavery was not a focus of my research. I was researching New Jersey, not the Southern states, so slavery would not even come up. Or so I thought.

But it did come up. It generally did not pertain to the specific things I was researching, but it would come up on the periphery. For example, I would come across the mention of slaves owned by families whose houses I was researching. These mentions occurred sporadically, but enough to make me realize that slavery was much more common in New Jersey than I had previously understood.

And then the realities of slavery in New Jersey began popping up in an unexpected place — the newspapers of the time.

Some of my research for the project involved reading through articles that appeared in New Jersey newspapers during the Revolutionary War era, looking for contemporary accounts of battles, skirmishes, politics, and other events. In the course of this newspaper research, I began to come across advertisements for the sale of slaves. Seeing these advertisements brought the reality of slavery in New Jersey right in my face in a more visceral way.

What was particularly chilling was how matter-of-fact these advertisements for the buying and selling of human beings were. They often read as if it were pieces of furniture or property being sold. In fact, there were times when the slaves were simply listed among other items of property being sold.

I have written in an earlier chapter that by spending so much time learning about the people who lived in New Jersey before me, I had developed a deep connection to them. I have a sense of relation to those who lived in my home state before me, even though there isn't a blood relationship. So for me, coming across these advertisements was like reading confessions of my ancestors' crimes.

Not only had these sales of human beings occurred in New Jersey, but the transactions had been handled publicly, unhidden, in the local newspapers, like it was just business as usual.

"What the hell were you people thinking?", I found myself asking them, down nearly two-and-a-half centuries. "How could you have thought this was morally acceptable?"

Of course, they couldn't answer me. Those of the past can't speak to us from their graves to give us answers or rationalizations to our questions or judgments. So if we choose to study history, and learn from it in a rewarding way, it is left to us to try to put the past in perspective.

A Search for Perspective

History is the story of what *did* happen, not what we wish had happened. Those who came before us were people of their times — times with views, standards, prejudices, and behaviors that were not as enlightened as ours. We can't change what they did or thought, but we can look to it to better understand and appreciate how our society and culture have developed into the present day.

We live in our own time, and we live by the standards of our time. We have the benefit of hindsight. We also have the benefit of living with the positive shifts in attitudes and behaviors that have occurred over the past several centuries. And — perhaps most importantly — we have the opportunity to learn from the actions of those who came before us.

Times change. Our society's views and standards will continue to change and (hopefully) advance over time. Those who come after us will look back and judge our time by their standards, and in some ways, we will not measure up.

I believe that it is a mistake for us to ignore or disregard the good done by our predecessors because of other things they did which we now consider wrong. However, I also believe that it is just as big a mistake to idealize historic figures and fully excuse their wrongdoings.

If we look to the past to find flawless heroes, we will be disappointed. What we will find instead are people who sometimes did good or great things, but who also did other things which fell short of those good things, or even stand in direct contradiction to them. In the case of the Revolutionary War era, it requires us to face the fact that people who expanded rights and freedoms for some, also did things to deny or limit those freedoms to others.

Like most Americans, I view our country as being rooted in ideals of equality, liberty, and freedom, so I know how painful and difficult it can be to try to reconcile the moral contradictions of our predecessors. For example, I have a very high regard for George Washington. I appreciate that he did many things — in his roles as soldier, stateman, and president — which advanced our progress toward a freer society. At the same time, I recognize that as an 18th Century Virginia plantation owner, he profited from owning slaves. Although it can be challenging, I hold these two seemingly contradictory ideas in my mind. I admire Washington for the enormous positive contributions he made, while never forgetting the other side of the story. For me, as an American, I will continue to view the Father of Our Country in high regard, while also continuing to hope that our country always moves forward to correct and atone for its past wrongs. I respectfully understand that others will see this matter differently, and some will come to conclusions different than my own regarding Washington and other founders. But the fact is that our predecessors helped create the society we now live in, good and bad. So there is always value in learning about them, even when some of what we learn is unpleasant.

To study the past is to be continually reminded of some hard realities — that human beings do contradictory things, that individuals are a mixture of good and bad, and that standards shift and change over time. This is part of what can make studying history fascinating and challenging.

To view history with the primary intent of either glorifying or denouncing the people of the past, is to diminish one's capacity to see it in all its complexity.

For me, the primary enjoyment of history is to simply learn what happened. Along the way, we are sometimes confronted with things we don't like, and painful contradictions we cannot reconcile. But we also give ourselves the opportunity to fully appreciate — and be challenged by — the study of the human story.

CHAPTER 20

RESEARCH DAYS - GOOD AND BAD

Researching history using primary sources involves days and days of reading through old documents to find the information you need. These documents can consist of letters, journals, newspapers, legal documents, and maps. You may be working with original copies, photocopies, reprints in books, or accessing them digitally.

This type of research is very much a solitary task, and it requires a personality that is comfortable spending long hours alone with your research. A certain amount of time is spent talking with librarians and archivists who can help you find the documents you need, but when it comes to the actual research, you are pretty much alone with those old documents. It can be a tedious and sometimes lonely process, but it is the best way to discover what happened in the past. It is the difference between just reading about history and truly researching it for yourself.

The Hunt

Researching a historical event is like a scavenger hunt. You want to know about something, and you try to locate the documents which will help you to learn about and understand it. Once you have those documents, you then hunt within the documents for the specific information you need.

For example, if you are researching a battle, there are important details you need to determine: Where did the fighting occur? Where were the generals headquartered? Who attacked first? And so forth.

To find the answers, you must first obtain as many relevant documents as you can from the time of the battle, such as the letters and military papers of the soldiers and officers, or contemporaneous newspaper articles about the battle. And then you are off on your hunt through the documents to find the information you need.

However, even if you are able to obtain every available relevant document, it is still possible that you will not find the information you are looking for. There are a number of reasons why this may happen: Information may have been recorded in a document that no longer exists. Or it may have been considered secret, and was only communicated verbally. Or it may simply never have occurred to anyone to write it down.

Things Unmentioned

Reading through old letters looking for certain information can sometimes be frustrating, because the people who wrote the letters may not have mentioned the details you are looking for. The letters were written between people who knew each other, and who therefore shared knowledge of certain day-to-day details which were obvious to both of them. People tend to not mention these types of details which are obvious to them. However, just because it was obvious to them, doesn't mean it is known to a researcher two-and-a-half centuries later. So as I read through the documents, I found myself wanting to ask some basic questions that weren't answered in the letters. Questions like: What did this person look like? What color was this house? How close was the house to the well?

These details might have been very important to my understanding of what happened, but they were such matter-of-fact details to whoever wrote the letter that it never occurred to them to mention it. And as much as I might want to ask them directly for the answers, that is obviously not possible. You can hope to get lucky and they'll mention what you are looking for, but there is no guarantee.

Information you don't find is one source of frustration you encounter while researching, but it is not the only one. Sometimes when you do find the information, it can get confused or jumbled. One way this happens is when different people had the same name.

The Name Game

In the 1700's, many members of an extended family often had the same first and last name. Not just parents and children, but also cousins, nephews, and other relatives. This can become very confusing, and it is the cause of headache-inducing frustrations to historians and genealogists researching that time period.

For example, I can recall one instance when I spent the better part of a day researching details about a particular soldier before I suddenly realized that I was mistakenly getting information about his father who had the same name. So I had to start over with researching the soldier. I was not happy. I had just thrown away an entire day without accomplishing anything useful, which meant that I had added one more day to the overall time the project would take.

The Balance

While there were many other frustrating days of research, there were days when it went smoothly. Sometimes I would just get lucky and quickly find the right documents to answer all my questions about whatever I was working on. Those days did not happen as often as I would have liked, but it was wonderful when they did. As the project progressed, I began to define my days as either "good research days" or "bad research days."

Ultimately, any such large research project will involve a combination of good and bad research days. Most likely the bad will outnumber the good. I say this in part to prepare anyone considering a large history project.

But I in no way want to discourage anyone from undertaking such a project! Because if you can make it through the bad research days, and stay determined to get the information as right as you can, you will feel rewarded when you do find what you were looking for. There were many times when I put together some information that I felt pretty confident had not been discovered before, and that by including it on the website, I was contributing to the world's historic knowledge. It is a great feeling.

There is always a need for more people who want to research and write about history based on solid research. So if you are up to the challenge of facing the bad research days — and sometimes many in a row — and are determined to stay focused on getting the information right, then dive in and enjoy the ride. The good research days will feel great, and the end result even better.

CHAPTER 21

PICK A CARD, ANY CARD

Some of my research days got very long. It was not uncommon for me to start working at five in the morning and end at eight in the evening. I would start to feel a little brain-dead by the end of those long days, especially when I was putting in multiple long days in a row.

One evening, at the end of one of those long days, I walked into a library that I frequented, to pick up some books related to what I was then working on.

The librarian at the desk asked me for my library card, and I opened up my wallet to retrieve it. But in my overtired state, I mistakenly handed him my ShopRite supermarket loyalty card instead! He looked at the ShopRite card with a confused look on his face, and then up at me. It took me a moment to realize what I had done, and then I gave him my actual library card.

He was polite with me, and didn't try to make me feel stupid. But still, I felt very embarrassed.

Over the course of the next several years of the project, I went back to the same library many times, and he was often at the desk. He was always polite, but I couldn't help wondering if he was thinking, "Here's that nitwit who thinks that this is a supermarket."

CHAPTER 22

WASHINGTON'S FOOTSTEPS

Over the course of the project, I spent an enormous amount of time physically following in George Washington's footsteps over New Jersey ground where he fought, encamped, advanced, and retreated. I was inside many of the houses in the state that he had been in, and I never got over the excitement of thinking, "Wow — George Washington was once in this room!"

I also spent hundreds of hours reading Washington's own words, written when he was in New Jersey. I pored over his letters and military documents to try to verify where he was and when, and trying to better understand his actions and experiences. Washington spent much of the war in New Jersey, and his actions were of great importance, and so he was the most regular focus of my attention. Through it all, he never ceased to intrigue and fascinate me. He remained consistently the person who most interested me during my research.

There are many scholars and historians who devote their entire career to studying Washington, and my knowledge and understanding of his life certainly do not come close to theirs. However, I do feel fortunate to have gotten a deep insight into one particular aspect of his life — his Revolutionary War experiences in New Jersey.

There are of course many other aspects to his life: surveyor, businessman, politician, statesman, president. All are interesting and worthy of study. However, during my work on the project, I needed to keep my focus on what he did in New Jersey throughout the Revolutionary War.

During the eight years of the Revolutionary War, Washington spent more time in New Jersey than anywhere else, and he spent it in many different parts of the state. As a result, I had a lot of Washington-related locations to visit and explore. What made it even more interesting was that he had spent time in the state at many stages of the war, and therefore was in many different circumstances and frames of mind during these times.

Washington first traveled through New Jersey early in the war, just after receiving the honor of commanding the Continental Army in June 1775. The following year, he traveled back across the state, but this time he was retreating with his army after a humiliating defeat. However, just weeks later, he enjoyed one of his great victories of the war when he crossed the Delaware River into New Jersey on the cold night of

Christmas 1776 to make a successful surprise attack on enemy forces in Trenton.

And so it would go until the end of the war — triumphs followed by humiliations, celebration intermixed with frustration — a great deal of which Washington experienced in New Jersey. By studying his times in New Jersey, I got to see him in a full range of experiences and emotions.

Given the amount of time that Washington spent in New Jersey during the Revolutionary War, and the important events which occurred here, it is fitting that the end of the war came while Washington was in New Jersey. On October 31, 1783, Washington was headquartered at Rockingham, NJ when he received news that the treaty which officially ended the Revolutionary War had been signed. Two days later, he wrote his Farewell Message to the army from the same location. And so it was in New Jersey that he got to savor his final victory, and reflect on the triumphs and disappointments of the war, many of which had occurred in this very state.

Just as Washington's New Jersey experiences spanned the length of the war, my own experiences in tracing his journey spanned the length of my project. The first historic location I photographed was the Holcombe House in Lambertville in September, 2009. Washington had stayed at the Holcombe House on two occasions during the war. The last place I visited, in February 2017, was the Kingsland Manor. Washington and his army had retreated along the Passaic River in 1776, less than a mile from Kingsland Manor.

In the seven-and-a-half years between those trips, I got to visit and explore many more Washington-related sites throughout the state. I spent a large amount of time reading what he had written, and spent even more time thinking about what he did, trying to better understand his actions and where they occurred. In some ways, Washington was my most constant companion during my years on the project. During that time, I always had some sense of awe about him. However, I neither idolized nor idealized him. As I discussed in Chapter 19, I understand that despite all his accomplishments and achievements, he was still an imperfect, flawed human being, and a man of his time. But I never stopped being impressed with the way Washington held the army together — under enormous pressures and through great difficulties — throughout eight years of war. When reading through his wartime letters, you can often feel his stress and frustration. But he never quite gives in to it. He never quits.

Some modern-day commentators like to put down Washington's skills as a general by saying that he wasn't a military genius, lost battles, and made some bad mistakes. While there may be truth to those claims, to me they miss the point. The fact is that Washington won the war. He was the head of the Continental Army for the length of the war, and went up against the awesome military power of the British Empire. At the end of eight years of war, he was still standing at the head of his army, and the British had been defeated. The Continental Army, led by General George Washington, had won the war, and secured American Independence.

There is a great lack of appreciation for the important role that New Jersey played in the Revolutionary War, and for the fact that Washington spent so much time here during the war. I would very much like to see this change, and in fact this was one of my motivations for creating the website in the first place. I hope that it has helped to change some people's perceptions, and to make them associate Washington with New Jersey.

George Washington is first and foremost associated with Virginia, and rightly so. He was born and raised in that state, and spent much of his life there. But in my mind and heart, he is also a New Jerseyan.

CHAPTER 23

A DAY IN THE LIFE

Over the course of the seven-and-a-half-year project, I took many road trips to explore and photograph historic sites. Throughout this book, I have mentioned incidents which occurred on some of them. In this chapter, I will focus on one entire day's road trip, which took place on September 25, 2013. I chose this day because it contains many of the elements which made these road trips fun and interesting, but also at times challenging and frustrating.

The Day

I was up and out by 6 a.m. I knew that it would be a long day because I had mapped out a plan that would take me to sites all over the state. I was anticipating about seven or eight hours on the road.

Because I was expecting a long day, I set out determined not to get sidetracked. I kept telling myself, "Stick to the locations I have mapped out for the day, and under no circumstances stop to investigate any location that isn't already on my list!"

My schedule for the day included locations in Salem, Cumberland, Cape May, Atlantic, and Ocean Counties, and would take me to rural areas, suburbs, shore towns, wilderness, and a city. I loved days like this because they allowed me to experience so many sides of New Jersey. My first scheduled stop was in Salem County — a church and cemetery in a rural town called Upper Pittsgrove. However, when I was a mile from that destination, I spotted a different old church and cemetery, one that I hadn't known about before.

"I have to check that church out," the curious side of me said.

"But I have to keep to the schedule," the practical side of me argued.

Not surprisingly, the curious side of me won out, and I spent about twenty minutes walking around the cemetery, finding some Revolutionary War soldiers' graves, and taking photos. So when I was done at that cemetery, I was already behind schedule, and I hadn't even reached my first scheduled stop. To make matters worse, the cemetery grass was wet with early morning dew, and my sneakers were soaked through. (This happened to me often, and I would always think that in the future I would take an extra pair of dry socks and sneakers with me, but at this point I had not actually started doing so yet.)

I got back in my car and drove a mile to the other cemetery in Upper Pittsgrove, the one that I had originally planned to visit. Even though my sneakers were soaked through, I enjoyed exploring it. I always liked visiting places like this in more rural areas, especially in the early mornings. I love being out among the trees and grass, and the peace and quiet.

From Salem County, I headed to a town called Millville in Cumberland County. I was behind schedule, and my feet were wet, but I was feeling happy and enjoying the sunny morning. I told myself, "Just don't get off the scheduled stops again!"

Millville was a suburban town that felt very different than the rural areas of Upper Pittsgrove I had just explored. I was in Millville to photograph a plaque on the municipal building related to a Revolutionary War officer named Joseph Buck. I took photos of the plaque and building, and then got back in my car, determined to stick to my scheduled stops. But as I drove away, I saw a sign for "Captain Joseph Buck Park." Since that was the name of the Revolutionary War officer on the plaque, the curious side of me wondered if there might be something to see and photograph inside the park. But the practical side of me said to keep going because I was already behind schedule.

Once again, the curious side of me won out, and I ended up glad that it did. The park was very nice, and I had it all to myself that early sunny morning. There was a great statue of Captain Joseph Buck in the park, along with a plaque telling his story. I spent extra time in the park after I had taken my photos, because I was enjoying walking around it so much.

By the time I get back to the car, I was feeling happy because my stops so far had been interesting and enjoyable. My sneakers were even starting to dry. But I was now over an hour behind schedule because of my unplanned stop, and I still had a lot of driving to do.

My next stop was also in Cumberland County, to a river known as Maurice River, the site of an obscure skirmish that occurred in August 1781. The riverbank was a quiet peaceful site tucked away behind a residential area. I enjoyed the spot very much, and it was another side of New Jersey that I got to see that day.

Next up was Atlantic County. One of the places I visited there was Estelle Park, which contains two historic cemeteries with Revolutionary War soldiers' graves. The park is very large and includes a nature center, and I found myself wishing I could just take the rest of the day off and spend it in the park. I didn't do that of course, but I did spend some extra time there exploring the park, which put me further behind schedule.

From there, I headed to Cape May County, where I was visiting a cemetery in South Dennis. The cemetery was pretty large, and it took me a while to find the grave I was looking for, putting me even further behind.

By this point, I had been to sites in multiple counties, and had spent time in rural and suburban areas, as well as shore towns. I had walked through cemeteries, parks, and nature centers. I had spent time at a secluded, peaceful riverbank. Next up was something entirely different — Atlantic City. But I wasn't there to gamble or see a show; I was there to photograph a historic sign dedicated to Jeremiah Leeds, a Revolutionary War veteran who was an early settler of what became Atlantic City. The sign was located on Atlantic Avenue, a street known to anyone who has ever played Monopoly. (The streets on a Monopoly board are based on the street names in Atlantic City.)

I took a closeup picture of the sign. The sun was shining from the right direction, and I got a nice clear photo I was happy with. But I decided that I also wanted to get a photo from further back, so that I could show the sign in the context of the surrounding area. The only problem was that in order to do so, I needed to take the photos from the middle of Atlantic Avenue, which is a busy street with a lot of cars speeding by.

So I waited for the red light to stop the traffic, ran out to the middle of the street, snapped a few photos, and ran back to the sidewalk when the light changed. However, when I was back on the sidewalk and could see the photos I had taken, I realized that the photos needed to be taken from a higher spot to look good. Usually, when I had a situation that required photos from a higher vantage point, I would use the ladder I kept in my trunk for such occasions. But in this case, I wasn't about to try running out in the middle of a busy street with a ladder to take the photos. (I did a lot of reckless, unsafe things to get photos over the course of the project, but even I knew it would be insane to try that!)

My solution was to wait for the next red light, run out in the street, hold the camera as high as I could over my head, try to point the camera in the right direction, take a few photos, and run back to the sidewalk before the light changed.

Unfortunately, because I couldn't see exactly where I was pointing the camera, I had taken a bunch of photos I couldn't use. So I repeated this process over the next several traffic light changes until I got a usable photo. I started to get self-conscious, wondering if anyone on the street was watching me, because I knew I must look like a nut. But I needed to get the photo, so I kept trying until I got it!

By the time I got out of Atlantic City, it was after 2 p.m. I had been on the road for over eight hours already, through multiple counties and vastly different parts of the state. But I wasn't done for the day yet, not by a long shot.

From Atlantic City, I headed north to Ocean County, where I had to stop at a local library which I knew had some research materials I needed. These were in-library reference items that were not available to be borrowed, so I would have to read through them at the library to determine what information I needed, and photocopy it.

This was a regular part of my research: going to libraries, reading through research materials to find what I needed, and photocopying it. But today was different. I had just spent more than eight hours driving all over the state, and so I was not exactly in the frame of mind to carefully read through research materials. But that is what had to be done, so I forced myself to get in the right frame of mind. I spent over an hour in the library and got the material I needed. The librarian was very helpful, as were all the librarians I worked with throughout the state during my work on the project.

When I left the library, I had a few more stops in the area to explore and photograph. And then I still had to drive another hour-and-a-half to get home. By the time I got home, it was almost 6 p.m. I had spent twelve hours on the road, and had gotten to experience widely different areas of the state in one day. I had experienced discoveries, delays, and distractions — the stuff that made the project so fascinating.

And this had just been one day out of so many.

CHAPTER 24

JERSEY

It is no secret that New Jersey is not the most highly regarded state. It is often used as a punch line. And despite the fact that it is rich in history, and that many notable people have lived here, it is generally not thought off as an important place.

This is certainly true of the public perception of the Revolutionary War. New Jersey is not a state that people generally associate with the Revolutionary War despite the important role that it played. This not only applies to people who do not live here, but unfortunately also applies to many people who *do* live here. In fact, my main purpose for creating the website was to do my own small part to remedy this situation by spotlighting just how important New Jersey's role in the war was.

Over the years of reading history, it became apparent to me that even knowledgeable history writers are susceptible to this New Jersey historical blind spot. Sometimes their wording will minimize New Jersey's important role, even as the story they are telling contradicts this notion.

Several years before I began the project, I was browsing in a bookstore, and started looking through Richard Brookhiser's biography of George Washington, skimming the early part of the book to see if I wanted to read it. On page 25, I came across a passage that really irked me — Brookhiser wrote that Washington spent most of the Revolutionary War in "a hundred-mile stretch between New York and Philadelphia," and he did not feel it was worth mentioning that this place had a name. In fact, it was not until three pages later that the words "New Jersey" are mentioned.

I was so annoyed with this "hundred-mile stretch between New York and Philadelphia" line that I put the book back and did not read any more of it. In fact, I have never read the book since then, nor any of Mr. Brookhiser's books.

I don't mean to single out Mr. Brookhiser unfairly. Even though I could not bring myself to buy or read any of his books, I have seen him interviewed on BookTV several times, and he seems like an interesting, knowledgeable historian and a nice guy. But that "hundred-mile stretch between New York and Philadelphia" line really stuck in my craw over the years. It was usually the example I would use when talking about the lack of respect New Jersey gets for its historical importance. In retrospect, I think it was one of the essential incidents which led me to deciding to undertake the *Revolutionary War New Jersey* project. In that regard, I do owe a debt to Mr.

Brookhiser, who lives on the stretch of island located to the east of the great state of New Jersey.

Beyond the lack of respect for New Jersey's historical importance, one finds an overall negative attitude about the state. It is often the butt of jokes. And as much as I love New Jersey, I understand that it is far from perfect, and that some of its imperfections are deserving of being joked about. However, while I might indulge in jokes or complaints about my home state with fellow New Jerseyans, I generally don't like hearing it from outsiders. I believe that this is similar to the way that most people feel about their friends and relatives.

At the same time, I can appreciate a Jersey joke — no matter who is telling it — if it is *actually funny*. To prove it, I would like to quote my all-time favorite Jersey-bashing joke, which appeared on the classic 1970's TV show *All in the Family*.

In one episode, Archie Bunker is hoping that his daughter Gloria and his son-in-law Mike "Meathead" Stivic will finally be moving out of Archie's house, now that Mike has graduated college. Mike and Gloria are having trouble finding an apartment in New York, and Archie is getting impatient. Archie tells Mike to, "Try Jersey."

Mike replies, "I *hate* Jersey!"

Archie responds, "*Everybody* hates Jersey, but somebody's gotta live there!"

CHAPTER 25

2014

Looking back on 2014, I can see that it was the year that the project began to crystallize and take on its final form. It may sound strange — and it feels strange for me to say it — but it took me about four-and-a-half years time and thousands of hours of work before I really understood the project's scope, and before I had found my way as a researcher.

The reality is that when I began the project, I had no formal training or experience as a researcher. During the first few years of the project, I went through a period of trial-and-error in learning to research, getting gradually better as I went along. I was actually training myself to do serious research, but I did not think of it that way at the time. However, with hindsight, I can clearly see this was the case.

Furthermore, the project was much larger than I realized or understood when I began, and it had grown consistently over the years. There had been an ongoing process of continually finding and adding new historic sites, causing the size and scope of the project to keep expanding.

But by 2014, things had started to fall into place, for a number of reasons. For one thing, I had finally come close to establishing the amount of towns and historic sites that would be included. Although there would continue to be some minor shifting and expanding of the number of historic sites right up until the completion of the project, I had now pretty much arrived near the final totals: about 230 towns, which included a total of about 650 historic sites.

Even more importantly, I had finally found my groove as a researcher. I had gone from originally obtaining information only from reference books and historic signs, to relying more and more on primary documents. I had also made great strides in learning how to locate these documents and how to best utilize them. I had learned the best places online for accessing historic documents and books. I had learned of the invaluable resources located at libraries throughout New Jersey, and had discovered how incredibly helpful the librarians are. After several years of "on-the-job training," I now felt comfortable and confident as a researcher. I can actually pinpoint the time when I realized that I was working with this newfound confidence as a researcher; it was a two-month period of March/April 2014 when I was working exclusively on research about Morristown. I can't exactly explain the change that had taken place, but something had definitely changed. After four-and-a-half years of research, I no longer felt like an amateur.

The project might have been an easier one if I had been trained for it, but then it would not mean as much to me. I have always been a self-teacher, and I enjoy the satisfaction that comes with it. I also think that I bring a different perspective to the work than if I had been formally trained.

As important as the research was, it was only one part of the project. Another large component was the driving trips that I took to visit, explore, and photograph the historic sites. I do not enjoy driving, and yet these driving trips which ranged from four to twelve hours had become a regular part of my life.

In the early years of the project, a friend of mine had taken many drives with me, starting with my very first trip in 2009. But by 2012, I was taking most of the drives solo, which meant spending a lot of time driving around in my car alone.

But by 2014, I had someone new to take on driving trips with me. Her name was Toni.

Toni began by taking occasional drives with me. Over time, she accompanied me more and more frequently, until eventually she was taking almost every drive with me. This made the driving trips much nicer.

Beyond the enjoyment of having friendly company and conversation on the drives, there were practical benefits to having someone with me. For example, there were often times when I had to park illegally to get near a location I was photographing, and it was helpful to have someone stay in the car in case it had to be moved. For another example, I sometimes had to climb to the top of my ladder to get a good photograph, and it was safer to have someone to hold the ladder steady to avoid falling.

Toni also brought another, more-important change to the project. She started reading everything I wrote for the website and giving me feedback. It quickly became an essential part of my working method — she would read each new draft I wrote, and would then give me her thoughts. She would patiently go through the same process over and over with me asking, the same questions: "Does it make sense?", "Is it easy to understand?", "Is it boring?" I began to trust her feedback more and more, and soon reached the point where I didn't consider anything I had written "done" until she said it was good.

I had seen interviews with a number of historians I admire who said they had someone in their life that performed a similar role for them, and how important it was to their process. Now I understood why.

****

As I stated at the beginning of this chapter, 2014 was the year that the project began to crystallize and take on its final structure. By the beginning of 2015, I knew approximately how many historic sites I would be including, and what they were. I had also developed the tools and skills I needed to properly research them. However, I still lacked an organized plan as to how to actually complete the project. Also, I still had not determined how much research was appropriate for each location, and therefore when to call a section "done." Because of these factors, I was to get a huge amount of work done in

2015, without ever really feeling like I was getting closer to finishing the project.

Over the course of the upcoming months, I felt the stress of working with no end in sight gradually increasing. I was still enjoying the ride, but as 2015 progressed, that stress got to me more and more.

I was still a long way from finished.

CHAPTER 26

IRON ORE NOT

The Revolutionary War, like all lengthy wars, was impacted by many things, including geography, geology, economics, weather, culture, and religion. Topics in each of these categories, and others, were at times part of my research. My interest level varied depending on the topic — some fascinated me, some engaged me somewhat, and some bored me. However, because I was continually moving from one topic to another, the overall variety usually kept me engaged, even when some things were less interesting.

Generally, I was most interested when I was learning about people. Some were ordinary local citizens whose lives became caught up in the war. Others were common soldiers who marched, camped, fought, suffered, and sometimes died in New Jersey. And others were famous Revolutionary War figures such as George Washington, Benjamin Franklin, Alexander Hamilton, and Aaron Burr. It was the human stories of all these types of people that kept me engaged through the seven-and-a-half years of the project.

On the other hand, purely military matters — such as weapons and uniforms — were of much less interest to me. When I had to research battles, I often found it tedious to have to learn the military details, such as all the commanding officers and their positions on the field. I was much more interested in the effects and significance of those battles, and the personal experiences of the soldiers and citizens involved in them. Those people stories balanced out the military details, so there was always something to engage me during my research of battles. I found this type of balance for most of the less-interesting topics I had to research.

There was, however, one topic that I truly hated — anything to do with iron. In the late 1700's, the mining of iron ore and the production of iron products were very important in New Jersey, both before and during the Revolutionary War. I could understand and appreciate that importance, but for some reason I just found it painfully boring. Unfortunately, it was a topic that came up somewhat regularly, and some locations I researched were entirely about iron production. Over time, I grew to hate working on anything related to iron. *Absolutely hate it.*

CHAPTER 27

JUST KEEP MOVING

One Sunday early in the project, I had planned a several-hour driving trip to photograph historic sites in Middlesex County. Unfortunately, I woke up that morning with an excruciating toothache. It hurt so bad that I didn't want to move. Because it was Sunday, I would not be able to see my dentist until Monday.

I considered just staying home to rest, instead of taking the driving trip. But then I thought, "I can lie here in terrible pain today and lose a day's progress, or I can drive around photographing in terrible pain and get a little bit further ahead in the project."

I decided to go.

That stubborn determination to just keep moving forward at all costs was typical of my behavior during the project. Another good example of this occurred on a winter day in early 2015.

A Cold Day in Hamburg

I had scheduled a day to drive to Hamburg, NJ to take pictures of a cemetery there, as well as the site of a Revolutionary War era iron works nearby. It was supposed to be cold that day, but it was also supposed to be a clear day, which is good for photographing.

Toni was taking the ride with me. When we got outside to leave, we discovered that it wasn't just cold, it was extremely cold. It was also very icy, and the locks on my trusty '94 Oldsmobile had frozen shut. But that wasn't enough to make me call off the trip — I couldn't lose a day's work!

So Toni and I spent about 45 minutes trying to unfreeze my car locks. I tried using a lighter to apply the flame to the lock, but that didn't work. (Being an older car, it didn't have an electronic remote car opener; it could only be opened manually with a key.)

Toni then said that vinegar was supposed to help unfreeze locks, so she ran in to get some vinegar, and she poured it repeatedly on the lock. But the vinegar didn't work either. Nothing we tried did.

Toni suggested that we take her car. She said that she didn't feel like driving, but that I could drive her car. We had some trouble with her car door as well, but it wasn't as frozen as mine, and we were able to get it open. We got in her car and headed out. As soon as I started driving, I heard that something in her car was running *really* loud. I became very concerned that the car would not make the two-hour drive to Hamburg and back on this cold, icy day.

"The car is fine," Toni tried to reassure me, "It always sounds a little loud." I still had serious worries, but that didn't stop me from going.

So we proceeded up Route 23 to Hamburg (which incidentally is a very nice New Jersey drive), but the whole time I was thinking, "I hope this car makes it there and back okay."

Along the way, Toni used her mittened hands to warm her face, which was freezing from all the time we had spent outside trying to open my car door.

"Whoa!," she said, "My mittens smell like vinegar!"

The Cemetery

We made it to the cemetery in one piece. When we got out of the car, it had gotten even colder. I am someone who likes cooler weather, and can generally handle the cold. I also wear shorts all year round, no matter what the weather, including that day in Hamburg.

But the cold that day was actually getting to me. It seemed especially cold in the cemetery, which is wide open to the wind, and Hamburg is at a high elevation. To top things off, I had forgotten my gloves, and I couldn't keep my hands in my pocket because I needed them to work my camera.

I knew that there were six graves in this cemetery of Revolutionary War soldiers, because I had read an article about them. My mission was to locate all six and photograph them. This turned out to be harder than anticipated. The cemetery was much bigger than expected, because there was a second section further back that wasn't visible from the entrance.

So I went looking for the Revolutionary War soldiers' graves. I had gone through this process many times at other cemeteries during the course of the project, but not in such cold weather with no gloves.

But there were graves to be found, so I started searching. Toni — helpful as always but with her mittens stinking of vinegar — walked around looking too. In the end, all six graves were found, and I photographed them.

We left the cemetery and drove a few blocks where I photographed the site of the iron works. We then headed home.

The car continued making a lot of noise, and I worried the whole way home if the car would make it. In the end, we got back without Toni's car dying.

Just another glamorous day in the life of a New Jersey historian.

CHAPTER 28

STOP AND LOOK AROUND

On my many drives exploring New Jersey, my primary task was to find historic places and discover the history behind them. Along the way I encountered many places of natural beauty, some of which were intertwined with the history itself.

One obvious example of this is the Great Falls of Paterson, which I have discussed in a previous chapter, but it is certainly not the only example. Although New Jersey is relatively small in geographic size, it contains a wide range of natural features — mountains, forests, and flatlands. There are also 130 miles of coastline, much of which consists of beaches on the Atlantic Ocean.

I have been familiar with the New Jersey shore for as long as I can remember, dating back to trips there with my grandparents when I was a kid. I have always appreciated the power of the ocean — its constancy, the crashing of the waves on the beach, and looking out towards the horizon where the curve of the earth causes you to lose site of the water where it meets the sky.

Wildwood Crest was one of the shore towns I went to when I was growing up. Decades later, in the course of my research, I discovered that a naval battle known as the Battle of Turtle Gut Inlet had occurred there on June 29, 1776, five days before the ratification of the Declaration of Independence. Turtle Gut Inlet, which gave the battle its name, was a thin body of water that ran through what is now Wildwood Crest. It no longer exists, because in 1922 it was artificially filled in.

After learning all this, I had a new appreciation of that piece of shoreline. Nothing about it had physically changed from before I learned its history, but now my appreciation for its physical features was enhanced by an understanding of its historical significance.

Not all of the beauty I encountered was part of the natural world; some of it was man-made. There were structures built with a practical, functional purpose, like houses, courthouses, and churches, which were designed and constructed beautifully. I also discovered some wonderful public art related to the Revolutionary War era, much of which were statues which can be found throughout the state, near where the history occurred.

My favorite of these statues is located in the Morristown Green. Known as "The Alliance", it consists of life-size depictions of Washington, Hamilton, and Lafayette. Because they are life-size and standing in a public park, they seem to invite interaction. Whenever I am at the Morristown Green, and I see people next to these statues, it makes me very happy to see how this piece of public artwork helps people to feel like they are physically interacting with historical figures. It is a great example of how art can help people to connect to history with an intimacy they might not otherwise feel.

One absolute must-see piece of Revolutionary War related public art is a mural on the side of a building in Trenton. Painted by Illia Barger, it depicts the public reading of the Declaration of Independence which took place in Trenton in 1776. It is painted in an effect which makes it appear three-dimensional and seems to bring the viewer and surroundings into the artwork. I highly recommend visiting Trenton to see this painting, which is called "Winds of Change," in person. No photo will do it justice. You really need to be physically in front of the painting to fully appreciate its effect.

****

There were times during my history explorations when I was totally absorbed in taking photos and finding information, and then something of beauty caused me to stop what I was doing and take notice. These moments gave me an important insight which I would like to pass on — if you are out looking for history, don't just get lost in the information. Take a moment to stop and look around. Don't hesitate to pause your learning to take in the beauty that may accompany the history you are looking at. This can intensify and multiply both experiences,

The beauty can help bring the history more to life, and the history can make a beautiful spot even more precious.

TEN RECOMMENDED PIECES OF REVOLUTIONARY WAR RELATED PUBLIC ART IN NEW JERSEY

Of the many worthy pieces in the state, this is a subjective list of ten that I happen to really like. (Listed alphabetically by town)

1. ***Thomas Paine* statue** — *Lawrence Holofcener, sculptor*
   Prince Street and Courtland Street / Bordentown, NJ

2. ***Rebelmen* statue** — *Carl E. Tefft, sculptor*
   Monument Park / Fort Lee, NJ

3. ***Captain Joseph Buck* statue** — *Gareth Curtiss, sculptor*
   Captain Joseph Buck Waterfront Park / Millville, NJ

4. ***The Alliance* statue group** — *StudioElS, sculptors*
   Morristown Green / Morristown, NJ

5. ***Patriot's Farewell* statue/fountain** — *Robert St. Croix, sculptor, fountain by R. R. Deskovick*
   Morristown Green / Morristown, NJ

6. ***George Washington* equestrian statue** — *Frederick George Richard Roth, sculptor*
   Morris Avenue, across from Ford Mansion / Morristown, NJ

7. ***Wars Of America* statue** — *Gutzon Borglum, sculptor*
   Military Park / Newark, NJ

8. ***Jonathan Witherspoon* statue** — *Alexander Stoddart, sculptor*
   Princeton University Campus / Princeton, NJ

9. ***Winds of Change* mural** — *Illia Barger, artist/muralist*
   South Warren Street / Trenton, NJ

10. ***Alexander Hamilton* bust** — *John Rapetti, sculptor*
    Hamilton-Burr Dueling Grounds Site / Weehawken, NJ

CHAPTER 29

THE DINNER QUESTION

A question commonly asked of historians is, "Which historical figure would you most like to have dinner with?" In my case, this would mean which of the Revolutionary War figures I studied during the course of the project.

George Washington might seem like my obvious choice, because he is the Revolutionary War figure who most interests me. However, I don't think that I would want to have dinner with him. It would probably feel just too intimidating to me to actually speak with him. On some level, I would like to experience for myself what his presence and bearing were like in person, but I think I would rather keep it a bit of a mystery.

My next favorite Revolutionary War figure, Benjamin Franklin, seems at first like a good choice, but upon reflection, not so. I have such a vivid image of Franklin in my mind —

always witty, always with something meaningful to say — that I would be afraid that he might not live up to my expectations.

Another possibility is Aaron Burr, who I think would be an interesting person to talk with. He seems to have had a particular charisma that drew some people to him strongly, but that made others dislike him intensely. I would enjoy the chance to observe his personality for myself. Also, my own opinion of Burr tends to be higher than that of many students of history. Whatever the experience might be of sitting and eating dinner with Burr, I am pretty confident that it would not be boring. However, as good a choice as Burr would be, I realize after some consideration that he would not be my first choice either.

The person who is my first choice is much less well-known than the three people I have just discussed. He is William "Billy" Lee, an enslaved person who was the personal servant of George Washington. Throughout eight years of the war, he was often the person nearest to General Washington, and so he was an observer and participant in an extensive range of Revolutionary War experiences — the triumphs and desperations, the battles and encampments, the victories and defeats.

William Lee spent time during the Revolutionary War at a number of the locations I researched for the project, and I always wanted to understand more about his experiences at those locations. Unfortunately, there are no known surviving documents written by him, so I never got the opportunity to see the events from his point of view. (It is unclear if he could read or write, and if so, to what extent.)

Apparently, William Lee took great pride for the rest of his life in the role he played in the Revolutionary War, and he enjoyed telling his war stories to visitors at Mount Vernon, George Washington's estate in Virginia. I would love the opportunity to hear these stories firsthand from him over dinner, and to hear about his feelings about his role in the war for Independence when he himself had not been independent. I would also very much like to understand how he viewed his relationship with Washington, because despite their slave/master situation, there does appear to have been some form of genuine friendship between them. It is hard to picture this from a modern standpoint, because the entire slave system seems incomprehensible now. (How could it have been considered acceptable to actually *own* human beings?) This makes me all the more want to hear William Lee's thoughts on the subject.

William Lee played an important role in the Revolutionary War, and he spent much of it in New Jersey. Because his words are absent from the documentary record, it may never be possible to fully understand and appreciate his role, but hopefully his name and importance will become better known someday.

Throughout the state, there are statues of some of the people who played an important Revolutionary War role in New Jersey. Washington is represented by many statues, and there are statues of Hamilton, Lafayette, Thomas Paine, Casimir Pulaski, and others. Perhaps someday there will be a statue of William "Billy" Lee in New Jersey. I hope so.

CHAPTER 30

THE PRESSURE BUILDS

By late 2015, I was really burnt out. I had been working on *Revolutionary War New Jersey* for over six years, and it had taken a toll on me. While there were still some things that I enjoyed about working on the project, much of the original excitement had faded. It had begun to feel like an obligation — something that I had put so much time and effort into, that I had to keep going to finish it.

The years of working long-hour days, with little time off, and no real vacations, were wearing on me. The project left me little time to do anything else. My attention to the details of the project had crossed over into obsession, and it took up most of my mental energy. As a result of these things, the project had started to overwhelm all the other aspects of my life.

I was beginning to tire of spending all of my time immersed in the Revolutionary War. I missed reading about other topics. I missed *thinking* about other topics! Most people find it surprising to hear, but the Revolutionary War is not my favorite topic. I happen to have devoted years of my life to it, but there are other subjects that I am more interested in, and the project was leaving me almost no time to pursue those other interests. I would try to fit in a little time before I went to sleep at night to read about things that weren't related to the Revolutionary War, but I just did not have the mental space left to seriously pursue anything else.

My financial situation was another source of stress. Because *Revolutionary War New Jersey* took up so much of life, I had little time and energy left for anything else. As a result, I was not generating much income with my web design business, and much of that income was immediately used up in basic living expenses, and the expenses of the project.

All of these stressors I was feeling from the project were becoming apparent to the people around me, and several of them expressed concerns about my well-being.

I could not continue on like this indefinitely. I needed to figure out a path to finishing the project, and stick to it.

The Plan

As 2015 came to a close, I took some time to assess what I had done, and what still remained to be done. I determined that there were sixty-six towns that I still needed to complete

work on. For most of those towns, I had done some preliminary research, so I would not be starting them from scratch. I
had also already taken many of the photos for those towns, so
the task ahead would mainly (but not totally) involve researching and writing, with much less driving and photographing
than had been involved before. However, there was still a lot of
researching and writing to be done for those sixty-six towns.

Nevertheless, I became determined to finish the project by
the end of 2016. I calculated I could do so by completing an
average of five-and-a-half towns a month for the next twelve
months. I knew that it would be very tough to maintain that
pace, and that it would involve me stepping up my already in-
tense work schedule, but I was determined to make it happen.

CHAPTER 31

2016 - THE FIRST HALF

And so I began 2016 with a plan. I had sixty-six towns left to complete. If I could maintain an average pace of completing five-and-a-half towns a month for the next twelve months, I would be done with the project by the end of 2016.

The year started off well. I completed a total of eleven towns by the end of February. This meant that I had met my goal of five-and-a-half towns a month for the first two months, so I was optimistic about maintaining that schedule for the rest of the year.

In March, my schedule fell apart. I have been blessed with good health for most of my adult life, and seldom get sick. I tend to go for years without getting a cold. But in March 2016, I got *really* sick with the flu. For one week, I literally got nothing done, because I just alternated between lying in bed or on the couch, feeling terrible.

Fortunately for me, I had Toni to come over to take care of me. Unfortunately for her, when I do actually get sick, I am a big baby about it. I must have been pretty annoying that week, because in between insisting that I was dying, I could only talk about how being sick was derailing my timetable to finish that year. At one point, I staggered to my computer to email Toni a link to the song "Seasons in the Sun," which she found very funny. But I'm not quite sure that I was entirely trying to be funny!

I felt slightly better the following week, but really was not up to getting anything done for *Revolutionary War New Jersey*. By the time I got seriously back to work on the project, I had not only lost two weeks of productivity, but it would take me a while longer to regain the energy I needed to put in long-hour days.

Because of the time lost while I was sick, I only completed three towns in March, which meant that I was now two-and-a-half towns behind schedule. I was discouraged and depressed by this, but I was determined to bounce back and get back on track. I moved through the next few months at a good pace, but never quite caught up to where I was supposed to be.

Countdown From Fifty

In mid-April, I reached a real milestone — I had fifty towns left to complete. Toni did a very nice thing for me at this point; she made me a kind of countdown calendar. It was like one of these customer number ticket things they use in bakeries, where they pull a number off and call out the next customer number. What Toni had done was take a small white pad and write the numbers from fifty down to zero in a stylish way, with something written or drawn on each page that was funny or encouraging. Having that pad on the wall, and the feeling of progress it gave me as I counted down, meant a great deal to me. I could *see* the progress I was making, and was reminded of it each time I passed by it. Each time I finished another town, it was a big moment for me to tear off another sheet and get down to the next number.

As I counted down from fifty towns, I started to get excited. I knew that I was getting closer to the end, and had a real plan for getting there. But as exciting as it was to be closing in on the finish, part of me had a hard time believing that I would ever actually be done. I would alternate between these two feelings on a regular basis.

As the spring months passed by, my enthusiasm for the project went up and down, depending on how difficult the research was, and the topic I was working on. When it was a topic I was not interested in (like anything to do with iron production) my days were not fun. But when I was researching something I liked, I enjoyed the work.

When it got to July, my research focused on one of my favorite topics of the entire project; I spent a considerable amount of time working on towns like Perth Amboy and Burlington, which involved the New Jersey experiences of Benjamin Franklin.

CHAPTER 32

BENJAMIN FRANKLIN'S NEW JERSEY

Benjamin Franklin is one of the most iconic figures of the Revolutionary War era. His face is probably more recognizable to most Americans than any other person from that time period, with the exception of George Washington. Many people have some sense of who Franklin was, even if they don't know details. However, one aspect of his life that is not generally recognized is his connections to New Jersey.

The Young Benjamin Franklin's Journeys Take Him Through New Jersey

Franklin was born in Boston in 1706, almost seven decades before the Revolutionary War began. At age twelve, he was apprenticed to his older brother Joseph's print shop. Young Benjamin learned the print trade there, and began his writing career by contributing to the newspaper *The Courant*, which Joseph published. However, Joseph mistreated Benjamin and even physically beat him, so at age seventeen, Benjamin ran away from his brother and his apprenticeship.

Franklin fled Boston by taking a boat to New York City, where he hoped to find work as a printer. He met a print shop owner in New York who told him there was no work for a printer there and advised him to seek work in Philadelphia. Benjamin took the advice and headed for Philadelphia via a route which took him through New Jersey; he took a boat from New York which landed in New Jersey at a spot known as the Bluff in Perth Amboy. The Bluff is still there for you to visit today, where you can try to imagine him arriving by boat in 1723, a half-century before the Revolutionary War began. Franklin was still years away from becoming the famous statesman and scientist known to history; he was then just a talented young man hoping to find work, and had no way of predicting the remarkable life he had ahead of him.

Neither Franklin nor anyone else could have foreseen the Revolutionary War or the important role that Franklin would play in it. It is important to always keep this concept in mind when studying history — that people who lived through events in the past never knew how the story would end. With the benefit of hindsight, *we* can know how their stories ended, but *they* could not foresee it. They lived each moment, each day, and each year of their lives uncertain of what the future would bring, just as we cannot predict our future. History comes alive much more when we keep this in mind.

From Perth Amboy, Franklin walked fifty miles across Central Jersey to Burlington, NJ, from where he could take a ferry across the Delaware River to Philadelphia. While in Burlington, he bought gingerbread from a woman, and lodged for the night in her house. The exact location of that house is not certain, but tradition holds that it was the Revell House, which still stands in Burlington. The following day, Franklin took a ferry to Philadelphia, the city where he would begin to build his fame.

During his years in Philadelphia, Franklin's business interests occasionally brought him back to New Jersey. Notably, in 1728, he was hired to print paper money for New Jersey, and the printing was done at 206 High Street in Burlington. That building no longer stands, but a sign at the site notes its history.

Over the following decades, Franklin's reputation grew as a businessman, writer, scientist, and statesman.

Benjamin and William Franklin — A New Jersey Father and Son Story

In 1763, Benjamin Franklin's son William was appointed the Royal Governor of New Jersey by the King of England. (The Revolutionary War was then still twelve years in the future, and New Jersey was therefore still a British colony.) William's first official Governor's residence was in Burlington;

later his official home was the Proprietary House in Perth Amboy, which still stands.

Benjamin and William were originally very close as father and son. As a boy, William had assisted his father in his famous kite electricity experiment. Sadly, due to the events of the Revolutionary War, that close father and son relationship was not to last.

As tensions began to increase between the colonies and Great Britain in the years leading up to the Revolutionary War, people began to choose sides. This unfortunately sometimes divided families, between those who wanted to remain Loyal to Britain, and those who supported American Independence. One of these many sad divided family stories was the Franklins. Benjamin chose the side of Independence, but his son remained Loyal to Great Britain. William's position had been granted to him by the King, so his decision to remain Loyal should not be surprising. Benjamin tried unsuccessfully to convince William to change his mind, which caused a rift between father and son.

Shortly before American Independence was declared, William Franklin, who as Royal Governor was a representative of the King of England, was arrested. Several days later, the Continental Congress voted to imprison William. To fully appreciate the drama of these events, it is important to realize that Benjamin was a member of the Continental Congress, and did not try to prevent his son's imprisonment.

Only weeks later, Benjamin traveled to Perth Amboy as part of a diplomatic mission with John Adams and Edward

Rutledge. They were to be taken by boat from Perth Amboy to Staten Island to discuss possible peace negotiations with British Admiral Richard Howe.

Along the way to Perth Amboy, they stopped for the night in New Brunswick. There was limited lodging available, so Franklin and Adams had to share a bed. Adams recorded the following story about that night in his diary: (Adams' spelling, punctuation, and capitalization have been left unchanged.)

"The Taverns were so full We could with difficulty obtain Entertainment. At Brunswick, but one bed could be procured for Dr. Franklin and me, in a Chamber little larger than the bed, without a Chimney and with only one small Window. The Window was open, and I, who was an invalid and afraid of the Air in the night [blowing upon me], shut it close. Oh! says Franklin dont shut the Window. We shall be suffocated. I answered I was afraid of the Evening Air. Dr. Franklin replied, the Air within this Chamber will soon be, and indeed is now worse than that without Doors: come! open the Window and come to bed, and I will convince you: I believe you are not acquainted with my Theory of Colds. Opening the Window and leaping into Bed, I said I had read his Letters to Dr. Cooper in which he had advanced, that Nobody ever got cold by going into a cold Church, or any other cold Air: but the Theory was so little consistent with my experience, that I thought it a Paradox: However I had so much curiosity to hear his reasons, that I would run the risque of a cold. The Doctor then began an harrangue, upon Air and cold and Respiration and Perspiration, with which I was so much amused that I soon fell asleep, and left him and his Philosophy together: but I believe they were equally sound and insensible, within a few minutes after me, for the last Words I heard were pronounced as if he was more than half asleep...."

The next day they were in Perth Amboy, from where they were taken by boat from the Bluff to Staten Island. This was the same Bluff where Franklin had arrived fifty-three years earlier as a young man, and only a few hundred yards from where his son had been arrested at the Governor's Mansion weeks before. What could have been going through Franklin's mind? What feelings could he have had? What memories flashed through him? Franklin was a man who kept his emotions below the surface, so it is unlikely that he let on to anyone what he might have been feeling.

Benjamin and William would only meet again once, years later, after the war had ended. Sadly, the rift in their father-son relationship never healed. Benjamin died in 1790, at the age of eighty-four; William died twenty-three years later.

****

Benjamin Franklin may not have spent a large portion of his life in New Jersey, but as we have seen, times that he did spend here were important and even life-changing for him.

New Jerseyans deserve to make more of a claim on the legacy of Benjamin Franklin. It is true that Franklin was born in Boston, and spent much of his life in Philadelphia, the city he is so closely associated with. But it is also true that several key moments in his life occurred in New Jersey.

CHAPTER 33

A GREAT MONTH
- AND THEN A
SAD DAY

I spent all of July 2016 researching locations associated with Benjamin Franklin. That made it one of my favorite months of the entire project. Franklin was such a fascinating person, that the time I spent studying him was a joy.

But as enjoyable as that time researching Franklin was, it will unfortunately always be associated in my mind with something sad.

In late July, I took a drive down to Perth Amboy to explore some sites associated with Franklin. Toni took the ride with me. It was a nice summer day, and we had a great time.

While we were driving home that afternoon, my car started to overheat on the Garden State Parkway. I pulled over onto the shoulder and called my mechanic Paul to ask him for advice. He was helpful and patient, as he had been for years whenever I had car trouble. He advised me to wait a while to let the car cool off, and then to drive with the heat on to pull heat away from the engine. He also said that I should try to avoid stopping, so as to not let the engine idle.

We waited until the car cooled down, and then started driving for home again. But I quickly realized that the overheating problem was much worse. The heat gauge needle was going all the way up *really* fast. I could not even make it to the next exit without having to pull over again onto the shoulder to let the car cool down again.

I needed to get us off the Parkway soon. It was getting later in the afternoon. I knew that if we got stuck in work traffic on the Parkway, the car would overheat for sure. So after letting the car cool down a bit, I headed for the next exit, which was less than a half-mile away.

I did make it to the next exit, but by the time I did, the temperature needle was going over the top. I was afraid that something very bad would happen to the car if I could not turn it off in the next few seconds. Luckily, I was able to quickly get off the exit, pull over on a local road, and turn off the car with the radiator still intact.

I checked and saw that the radiator was completely empty, so we started walking to find someone to ask for water. We found a man named Mike, who was friendly and helpful. He went into his house, and came back out with several plastic containers filled with water. We thanked him, walked back to the car, filled up the radiator, and then drove the backroads home. Fortunately, we had water left over to take with us, because the car started to overheat again on the way home, and we needed to stop and refill the radiator.

Overall, the trip home had taken over three hours, instead of what normally would have been a forty-minute drive. But we didn't let the bad experience on the drive home ruin what had been a great day. The trip home was one of those things that feels annoying when it is happening, but afterwards feels like it was an adventure.

I dropped the car off at Paul's garage a couple of days later. It was after hours, so I did not actually see him. I just left my car with the keys. He called me the next day to tell me that the car definitely needed a new radiator. He had ordered one, but said that it might-take a few days before it arrived.

Meanwhile, I went on working on the towns associated with Benjamin Franklin, which I finished on the last day of July. It had been a great month. Even though I had only finished three towns in July, and so had fallen farther behind schedule, the month had been very enjoyable because of the subject matter.

I began August in good spirits. I called Paul on the afternoon of August 1, to ask about the status of my car. He told me that he was still waiting for the new radiator to come in, and it might take several days.

I called Paul back a few days later, to see if the radiator had arrived. Someone answered his phone, but it was not Paul — it was the voice of someone I had never heard before.

I immediately sensed that something bad had happened. It turned out to be Paul's son on the phone, and he informed me that Paul had gone to the hospital on the night of August 1, and died there on August 2. I was completely shocked; Paul had sounded fine when I spoke with him on the afternoon of August 1. I explained to his son how helpful Paul had always been to me, and how much I had liked him.

I went to pick up my car in the parking lot of Paul's garage several days later. Based on my last conversation with Paul — when he had told me that he was still waiting for the new radiator to arrive — I expected that my old radiator would still be in the car. With that in mind, I had purchased a bottle of radiator leak repair liquid at an auto parts store. I hoped that it might buy me a little time until I could find a mechanic to install a new radiator.

However, when I opened up the hood to pour in the radiator leak repair fluid, I saw that there was a new radiator installed. I was completely baffled by this. I could not understand how the new radiator got there; I was already feeling a bit stunned by Paul's unexpected passing, and this just compounded it.

But after giving it some thought, I realized what must have happened. Apparently, the new radiator was delivered to Paul's garage *just after* I spoke with him on August 1, and he installed it *right away*. He must have started to feel ill soon after that and went to the hospital.

My Oldsmobile, which had originally belonged to Paul's mother before he sold it to me, was apparently the last car he worked on in this life.

Paul's death was the saddest moment of the project. He was a great guy who had always gone out of his way to keep my old car running. He regularly did work for me on credit, as he was understanding about me not having the money to pay on time.

In practical terms, his contribution to the project was invaluable. He helped keep my old car running to continue driving around the state to research and photograph. I would often stop by his garage before I had to make a particularly long drive for the project, just to have him look over the basics of my car, and he wouldn't even charge me.

He had spoken with me about the project with interest many times, and had given me positive feedback after looking at the website, which was always nice. We always laughed a lot.

If my car had not overheated on the way back from Perth Amboy, I would most likely not have gotten to speak with him those last few times. So in that respect, I'm grateful that my radiator busted when it did. It is unfortunate that I did not get to actually see him again.

Because of the timing of Paul's death, I will always associate him with Benjamin Franklin. I think that he would have gotten a laugh about that.

I miss him.

CHAPTER 34

2016 - THE SECOND HALF

I moved into August with mixed feelings. I had begun the month six-and-a-half towns behind schedule, and I knew that it would be hard to catch up and complete the project in 2016. On the other hand, I was continually making progress, and moving slowly but surely towards the finish line. I was still dealing with the conflicted mindset I described earlier. One minute I would feel optimistic excitement, and the next I would despair that I would never reach the end. The month ended up going well, and was very productive. However, even in my happier moments, I still had an underlying sadness in me over Paul's death, which had been as unexpected as it was sad. It was to affect me for some time.

Twenty-Five to Go

On September 2, I reached the milestone of having twenty-five towns to go. This was a big deal! I still had the occasional feelings of "I'll never actually finish," but my excitement and optimism were beginning to push those feelings aside.

To commemorate reaching twenty-five towns to go, Toni and I danced to the song "In the Year 2525" by Zegar and Evans. This began a new tradition we would do for most of the remaining towns as I counted down — we would commemorate town completions by dancing to a song related to the number of towns I had left. I really can't dance well, and some of the songs were not exactly dance songs. But we had fun and laughed a lot, which is all that really mattered.

Getting Closer

On Halloween, I reached a huge milestone — ten towns to go! I was very happy and excited about getting so close to the end. Appropriately, we danced to the song "Getting Closer" by Wings to commemorate the occasion.

Counting down from ten made the possibility of finishing feel very real. I had gone through years of work on the project with no idea when or how I would ever reach the end. But now the finish line was clearly visible; my skepticism about actually reaching it still flickered but much less so than it had before.

On Thanksgiving, I reached the ultimate milestone — five towns to go! At that point, all lingering feelings of "I'll never actually finish" were gone. However, I took stock of the five towns I had left, and realized that each of them would require an exceptional amount of research, and so I would not be able to complete the project by the end of the year. It would most likely take me until February or March. This was a disappointment, but one I could live with.

When 2016 drew to a close, I had only four towns left to go. I was very close to the end.

CHAPTER 35

"IT'S GETTING VERY NEAR THE END" - Early 2017

As the New Year began, I felt good about how close I was to completing the project. There was some disappointment that I had not finished in 2016, but the fact that I was within reach of the end made it OK. I only had four towns left to go, which I estimated would take two or three months, so I knew that this would be the last New Year I would see with the project unfinished.

I was able to complete three of those towns by the end of January, which left me with only one more town. When I pulled the page off the countdown calendar Toni had made me, and saw the page reading, "One town to go," I could hardly believe it.

The last town I had to complete was Nutley. As was the case with many of the towns, I had done intermittent preliminary research for Nutley over the past few years, but now it was time to dive deep into the information and tie it all together.

As I worked on Nutley throughout February, I felt an odd combination of emotions. I was of course excited by the thought of finishing the project, but I was also nervous. My life would soon be very different — I would no longer get up each morning thinking about how much more *Revolutionary War New Jersey* was left to do. As much as I was looking forward to that, it was a little scary. I had been working on the project for seven-and-a-half years, and even though I had grown somewhat tired of the routine, it had become a familiar way of life to me. And that was going to change soon.

One of the historic sites I researched for Nutley was the Kingsland Manor. I have a vivid memory associated with the Kingsland Manor that perfectly illustrates the bittersweet feelings I had about finishing the project. On February 19, the Kingsland Manor's curator Leon Kish gave me an in-depth tour of the house, and shared some historic documents with me. Leon could not have been more helpful. He took me through each section of the house and described its long and interesting history for me. Actually, much of the historical interest of the house was from times after the Revolutionary War, and so would not factor into my project, but I was interested by all of it. At the end of our time, Leon and I were talking in the basement of the house, part of which had been used as a speakeasy in the 1930's. We were having a long conversation, which I was enjoying very much. And then in the back of my mind it occurred to me that this was all coming to an end. There would be no more touring interesting places and interviewing friendly, knowledgeable people. No more exploring every corner of New Jersey. As much as I had been looking forward to finishing the project, I now also felt a bit sad about leaving it all behind.

Kingsland Manor ended up being the last place I visited and photographed for the project, and Leon was the last person I interviewed.

I completed the Nutley page on February 24. I tore the next page off the countdown calendar Toni had made me, just as I had done for the last fifty towns. But this time there was no number on the page. It read, "And then there were none." It was mind-blowing — I had no more towns to work on!

I was done with the research. I was done with the photos. Best of all, I was done with the driving!

However, I was not totally done with the project. I still had to write the Home and About pages of the website, which would take a few days of work. But those pages were basically introductory pieces which would require no research. The hard work of researching and documenting the Revolutionary War history of 230 towns was now behind me. I had looked forward to this moment for years, but on some level, I had never truly believed it would happen. Now it was here. I needed to just sit alone and let it all sink in, before I tried to communicate my feelings to anyone.

I decided to go out and pick up some food and then find somewhere pleasant to eat it. When I left, I don't think that

I even had a plan of where I was going. I ended up at Blaze Pizza, where I ordered two personal-size vegan pies — one with mushrooms and one without — and headed to a nearby park which the Passaic River flowed through. I parked my car and walked through the park to the riverside with the pies and a bottle of water.

There had been some unseasonably warm days, and it reached seventy degrees that afternoon, which is highly un-usual for February in New Jersey. It was a great afternoon to sit by the river and eat. Memories flowed through my mind of seven-and-a-half years of exploring New Jersey — its towns and cities, its houses and museums, its churches and cemeteries, its mountains and rivers (including the Passaic River, which I was sitting at). It was an overwhelming emotional experience to realize that the process of exploring and researching 230 towns was over. I knew that I would likely do other history research projects later in life, but I also knew for certain that I would never undertake anything so large in size and scope again.

I sat by the river for about an hour, just letting my thoughts flow and adjust to the change. When I got up to head home, I was feeling happy.

Unfortunately, Toni was in the midst of the flu at the time, so we didn't get to dance and celebrate that night. But that was OK, because there would be even bigger cause to celebrate in a few days when the entire project would be finished. I was eager to get to that finish line, so at 5 a.m. the next morning, which was a Saturday, I sat down to begin work on the About page, one of the two remaining pieces I had to write.

The purpose of the About page was to briefly describe my experiences of working on the project, and also to thank those who had been of help to me. There were the friends and family who had given me encouragement over the long course of the project, as well as the librarians and archivists who had provided such invaluable assistance in locating documents. I felt happy to be writing these Thank Yous, and I was looking forward to completing the project so that I could ask those people to go and read my Thank Yous for themselves. My biggest Thank You went, of course, to Toni, followed by my Mom, who I dedicated the website to.

I completed the About page text over the course of a few days. On the morning of February 28, I began working on the Home page, the final piece I had to write. It was just to serve as a basic intro to the website, and would only be about five or six paragraphs, so I thought it would be an easy write. It wasn't. I spent the day doing multiple drafts, and getting frustrated with what I was writing. In retrospect, I can see that I was feeling nervous about actually closing the lid on the project, so I was overthinking what I was writing.

By the end of the day, I had a pretty good draft of the Home page, but I was still trying to get my mind to accept the idea of finishing the project.

It was the last day of February. I knew that I could finish the Home page, and therefore the entire project, the next day if I really wanted to, but I was still processing the thought of actually doing so. I went to sleep thinking that the next day might be the completion of the project, but I was unsure if I would actually make it happen.

CHAPTER 36

THE LAST DAY

I woke up on March 1 feeling nervous, almost to the point of feeling sick. I knew that I was so close to the end that I could possibly finish the project that day, but I did not know for certain that I would. All of the mixed emotions I had felt over the past few weeks had kicked into high gear.

I began work at 6 a.m., and spent several hours working on the Home page text that I had begun the day before, pausing only for a half-hour to exercise. This should have been a very easy piece of writing, but I was finding it difficult, and I was getting frustrated.

Around 10 a.m., I called Bob Thompson, a history writer I know, to discuss the difficulties I was having. I sent him my latest draft of the Home page. He read it and told me he thought it was good, and with that reassurance, I went back to work.

Unfortunately, I also went back to going in circles. I made a series of minor adjustments to the Home page text, asking

Toni to read each one. She kept telling me it was good, but I was convinced that there was something wrong with what I had written. I was feeling more and more nervous and sick to my stomach.

I decided that I needed to get out for a while to clear my head. Toni happened to have a dental appointment that afternoon, so I offered to drive her. I tried to work on the text in my car while I waited for her during her appointment, but my nervousness was making it hard for me to focus. Next, I drove her to Petco. She was in the store for quite some time, and it gave me time to think as I sat in my car in the parking lot.

And then suddenly it hit me — I did not want go to sleep another night with the project unfinished. I saw very clearly that I had been dragging my feet unnecessarily since I got up that morning. But now I needed to stop procrastinating, so that I could finish the project *that day*. Instantly, the nervousness and sick feeling left me, and I felt focused. I was now committed to completing the project by the end of the day.

As soon as I got home, I made a quick round of tweaks to the Home page text to finish it, and then emailed it to Toni who told me it was good. With that, all of my writing for the project was completed. It was around 3:30 p.m.

There were still a few things to be taken care of before I could call the entire project "done." The first was to send out the Home page for a final proofread for grammar and punctuation. I emailed the page to Joan Barret, who had done the final proofread of my pages for the past several years. I explained that this was the last thing I would ever need proofread for the project. Right after I sent it, I got very nervous. It suddenly occurred to me — what if Joan was busy, or sick, or away, and would not be able to get to it right away? That would mean that I could not finish the project that day. As it turned out, I had nothing to worry about. She emailed me right back saying that she would get to it shortly.

I had to wait for a while, and there was nothing else I could do for the project until I had the proofreading done, so I started watching an episode of the 1974 *Planet of the Apes* TV show, online. The show had been a childhood favorite of mine, and getting near completion of the project put me in a nostalgic frame of mind. However, I did not get to watch the entire episode, because I received an email back from Joan at 4:30 p.m. with the proofread marks. There were just two commas to be fixed, so it only took me a minute to make the corrections.

I still had a few technical odds and ends to take care of, the last of which would be backing up all of the project's digital files to an external drive. These things would only take me a few hours at most, so I knew that I would definitely be finishing the project that night.

I called Toni to tell her that I would be done soon, and that I would call her back to come over then. However, I also told her that when I called her back, I would not say that I was done over the phone. After all these years of work, I would want to tell her I was done in person, face-to-face.

Shortly after 6 p.m., I finished backing up all the project's digital files to the external drive, and then locked the external drive in a fireproof metal box. I put the metal box on the shelf behind me, and then turned around to see that the clock on my computer read 6:11 p.m. The project was completed.

I called Toni back and asked her to come over. When she arrived, I said something like, "At 6:11 p.m., after seven-and-a-half years, and ten thousand hours of work, I finally completed *Revolutionary War New Jersey*." It felt great to say it out loud.

We then danced to a batch of songs whose titles or lyrics were somehow relevant to me completing the project, interspersed with me making calls to people to tell them that I had finished. Toni had just gotten over the flu, and was still feeling tired and not great, so I really appreciated her dancing for a while to celebrate with me.

The songs we danced to included: "I" (KISS); "Revolution" (The Beatles); "This Town" (The Go-Go's); "Let's Have A War" (Fear); "Circle Sky" (The Monkees); and "Long Title: Do I Have To Do This All Over Again?" (The Monkees). We then listened to The Beatles, *Abbey Road*, Side Two Medley, which culminates in the song "The End."

Later on that night, I watched the rest of that *Planet of the Apes* TV episode. It may seem like not a particularly exciting thing to do on such a special night, but in its own simple way it was. For the past several years, whenever I took time to do anything relaxing, unproductive, or fun instead of working on the project, I always felt a bit guilty, but not this night. My time was now my own, more than it had been in years, and that made even the smallest things seem special.

The project was done, and I felt fantastic. The feelings I had that night will never be equaled for the rest of my life. Although I will work on and complete other projects, I know now — and I knew then — that I would never attempt anything so large in scope ever again.

I went to sleep that night feeling great, with no thoughts in my head of what needed to be done tomorrow for *Revolutionary War New Jersey*. I slept more soundly than I had in years. I was done.

CHAPTER 37

AFTER THE END

The next morning, I woke up to a whole new world. For the first time in years, I did not have to think about what needed to be done for *Revolutionary War New Jersey*.

It was a Thursday morning. I decided to take the next four days off from any responsibilities. I put "Al is away until Monday" messages on my web design business voicemail and email, so that my relaxation could go completely undisturbed.

The first thing I did was go to Super Cuts to get my hair cut. Back in 2014, I had decided to stop cutting my hair and just let it grow until the project was done. By now it had grown very long, so having it chopped off was an instant big change. I felt like a new man. It was a good way to start things off in a new direction.

It would have been nice to take a big trip to celebrate, but the years of focusing on the project had left me without the money to make that happen, so Toni and I had fun locally. Over those four days, we did the kind of things I had not had much time for while working on the project. We went out to play miniature golf, air hockey, pool, ping-pong, and went bowling. These may sound like small things, but to me they felt huge. Just to have four days of free time to enjoy — without thoughts of *Revolutionary War New Jersey* in the back of my mind — felt amazing.

On Monday morning, I settled in to my new reality. I focused my attention on getting caught up on the many things that had been put on the backburner while my life was devoted to *Revolutionary War New Jersey*. But that still left me much more free time than I had had in years, which made me very happy.

Over the next few weeks, I made calls to thank people who had helped me in some way with my research, or who had provided ongoing encouragement during the project. I enjoyed this process, especially when it was someone I had mentioned in the Acknowledgements section of the website. I felt happy asking them to go read where I had thanked them.

To commemorate my completing the website, my Mom bought me a telescope as a present. It is a large Dobsonian reflector telescope, and Toni and I joked that it looked like a rocket launcher. I had been to observatories before, and found astronomy interesting, but I had never actually owned a telescope, so I really appreciated the gift. The first night, we got to see Saturn, Jupiter, and the waning crescent Moon through the telescope, which was a great start. There have been many more good times with that telescope, and I look forward to more in the future. It will always feel extra special to me because it was a commemoration of finishing the project.

Twelve days after finishing the project, my family had a party for me, which was very nice. In general, the congratulations I got from people at this time was heartwarming.

For the next seven months, I took completely off from anything to do with the Revolutionary War. I didn't read about it, I didn't talk about it, and for the most part I never even thought about it. I knew that at some point I would be doing another project to follow up the website, but I was not in any hurry to get to it. I needed the break.

I was enjoying my free time in different ways. I was particularly happy to be able to read whatever I wanted, and caught up on some novels I had wanted to read for a long time.

Toni and I took a trip to Binghamton, New York because it was the hometown of our mutual hero Rod Serling, the creator of the *Twilight Zone*. It was the first trip I had taken that was not related to Revolutionary War research since before I began the project. In fact, it was the first time in several years that I had left New Jersey at all. It was fun to visit places associated with Serling. It felt particularly liberating to explore a place without having to then write about it.

By the fall, I started thinking that at some time soon I would be returning to the Revolutionary War. Most importantly, I wanted to somehow turn what I had done into a book. I was proud of the website, but I very much wanted to do something in book form. I have always been a book lover, and I value physical copies much more than anything digital. But I wasn't quite ready to return to working on the Revolutionary War.

The first crack in my reluctance to reconnect with the Revolutionary War came in October, when I took my friend Anthony to breakfast in Morristown for his birthday. After we ate, I took him to a few of the many Revolutionary War sites in Morristown and talked with him about the historic events that had occurred at them. It was the first time since finishing the project that I had visited a Revolutionary War site, or had even talked about the topic. I found that after taking a half-year complete break, I had a new-found enjoyment in being back at these sites, and talking about them. The next month, I found myself back in Morristown with another friend, Dennis. Once again, I found myself playing the same role of showing the historic sites and talking about them, and once again I enjoyed it. I was easing myself back into the Revolutionary War.

After the New Year, I sat down to figure out what type of Revolutionary War book I was going to write. I made a list of eight ideas for the book, and then spoke with people to get their feedback to those ideas. I was surprised to hear that what they were most interested in was my own experiences in creating the project. This had not been on my list of possible book topics, and honestly it had not even occurred to me before.

However, the idea did appeal to me for several reasons. First of all, it would be a big change of pace from the writing I had done on the website, where I had tried to keep myself out of the picture as much as possible. Also, it would not require any new research on my part. I began to envision writing the book you have been reading, and I quickly decided that it was absolutely the form the book would take.

I soon made another decision that was equally important — that I would not write the book on a computer. This idea thrilled me. Although I have made a living designing websites, and the *Revolutionary War New Jersey* project was itself a website, I do not really like modern technology, and I am happier when I am not in contact with it.

Having decided not to use a computer, I needed to figure out how I would do the writing. I considered writing the book by hand, or dictating it into a tape recorder and having it transcribed. Then I remembered that my Mom had an old typewriter when I was growing up. I gave her a call and asked if she still had it. She said it had not been used in decades, but she had kept it in the basement in case anyone ever wanted it.

A few days later, I was at my Mom's house, and I went down to the basement to try the typewriter. I set it up on a table and typed a few words. Remarkably the ink on the ribbon had not dried up in all the years it had sat unused in the basement. I knew instantly that I would use the typewriter to write the book. I was so immediately attached to typing on a typewriter that I knew that I would use one for the rest of my life. I walked up from the basement and said to my Mom, "I think I'm in love!", referring to the typewriter.

It is a Royal Quiet Deluxe manual typewriter, made in 1947. It is built into its own carrying case, with a hinged lid that opens and closes, which makes it easily portable. It had originally belonged to my great-aunt Stephanie, who had been a secretary. At some point, she gave it to my Mom, who had herself worked as a secretary from 1952-55. I loved everything about the typewriter, and the fact that it had a family history dating back seven decades made it even more special to me.

I had known that there were writers who still used typewriters, but now I understood why firsthand. I enjoy the fact that not using a computer means that I do not have the ability to change font styles and no way to drag and drop sentences and paragraphs around. I find that these restrictions mean that I am more focused on the actual words as I am writing. The editing process involves the typed pages, a pencil, an eraser, white-out, scissors, and tape. And then a new draft requires actually retyping the pages. I personally love this old-school, labor-intensive method of writing, but I realize that it is not for everyone. I recommend that if you have access to a typewriter, give it a try. You'll know right away if it is for you.

With the typewriter, the last piece of the puzzle was in place, and on March 1, 2018 — a year to the day since I finished the website — I began writing the book you have just read.

I have enjoyed writing this book more than I could have imagined. It was a pressure-free project that gave me a creative freedom that the website did not. More importantly, it allowed me to mentally and emotionally relive those seven-and-a-half years of exploration, and to appreciate them on a whole new level. I feel very grateful to have had the opportunity to so thoroughly explore my home state, and to have created something that has helped so many people learn its history for themselves. The *Revolutionary War New Jersey* website project was a tremendous experience that I will always cherish. I hope that you have enjoyed my story.

ACKNOWLEDGEMENTS

Writing this book was a very different process and experience than creating the website. However, one thing that remains the same is my appreciation for those who have encouraged and helped me.

My biggest thank you goes to my fiancée Toni. In addition to all of her love, support, and encouragement throughout the writing of this book, she also played an invaluable role as my editor. Toni read over each of my drafts, offering suggestions on how to polish the text. She had played the same role during the last several years of the website project, but it took on even greater importance with the more personal writing style I was attempting with this book. I thank her for the time and effort she put into helping me, and above all for the joy she brings to my life.

I did a considerable amount of the writing of this book at my Mom's house in her quilting room. It is a great room to write in, with good natural sunlight most of the day. It helped me to completely focus on what I was writing, as I sat typing at a small desk, surrounded by my Mom's artwork on the walls.

We enjoyed many lunches and dinners together on the days I worked there, and she provided ongoing encouragement for what I was writing. I thank her for all this, as well as the many other things that make her a great Mom.

Throughout the time I was writing this book, I regularly discussed it with my friend Dennis Harry, and on several occasions, he read drafts of what I had written and offered feedback. Dennis also played another important role in the process. Before I began writing the book, he asked me if could go with him to some of the historic sites that I had researched for the *Revolutionary War New Jersey* website, and tell him about their history. I said that I would be happy to, as long as he drove. (After completing the website, I try to avoid any unnecessary driving.) We took a number of such road trips, which helped me mentally reconnect to my experiences during the website project, and therefore made it easier to write about them. Thank you Dennis.

My friend Chris Magenta was a great source of support and encouragement throughout the seven-and-a-half years of the website project, and remained so during the time I was writing this book. Our conversations are an important part of my life. The funny thing is that as much as he is a supporter of my history work, we rarely discuss the Revolutionary War. Instead, our conversations often give me a mental break from what I am working on, and usually focus on our other shared favorite topics, including the Beatles (especially how great Ringo's drumming is), Watergate, classic films, *The Twilight Zone*,

1990's politics, silver and bronze age comics, and *Columbo*. I am fortunate to have him as a friend.

Thank you to Ashley Ziccardi, Blake McGready, Bob Thompson, Scott Dambrot, Joe Lilore Sr., Anthony McCauley, Dr. Jon Heller, and Dave Meredith for the times they each took to discuss what I was writing, and the encouragement and feedback they provided.

I would also like to acknowledge my brothers, sisters-in-law, nieces, and nephews-in-law. At one time or another during the time I was writing this book, I talked with each of them about what I was working on, and they offered their encouragement. A special thank you goes to my niece April, who took the time to read a near-final draft of this book and give me feedback.

I remain forever grateful to the many librarians and archivists throughout New Jersey who helped me to locate and access documents during my research for the website project.

I also remain grateful to Paul Alexander, Paul Bonazzi (R.I.P. August 2, 2016), and Joan Barrett. Each of them provided help to me during the website project which is mentioned within the narrative of this book.

I would also like to thank Stephanie Kip, Tracy Stoft, and Jo and Kat Lilore.

Finally, thank you to Michele Marra for loaning me a typewriter when my Royal Quiet Deluxe typewriter needed repairs, and to Albert Kren for the quick, professional, friendly service he provided when he repaired my Royal Quiet Deluxe.

CHAPTER NOTES

The historical information in this book is based chiefly on the years of research that went into creating the *Revolutionary War New Jersey* website. Because this book is mainly focused on my own experiences, it contains much less detailed source notes than those that appear on the website, which was focused entirely on history. In some instances in the following chapter notes, I specify the relevant page(s) on the website where you can find further information and detailed source notes about historic events mentioned in this book.

The descriptions of my own experiences which appear in this book are based on detailed notes and calendars I kept while I was working on the *Revolutionary War New Jersey* website project, along with my own vivid memories.

CHAPTER 1 / REVOLUTIONARY WAR NEW JERSEY

No Chapter Notes

CHAPTER 2 / BEFORE THE BEGINNING

The title of this chapter is an homage to the film *Citizen Kane*, drawn from the following dialogue:

Thompson: "After all, you were with him from the beginning."

Bernstein: "From before the beginning, young fellow. And now, it's after the end."

Screenplay by Herman J. Mankiewicz and Orson Welles.

Produced and Directed by Orson Welles.

Released 1941.

CHAPTER 3 / GETTING STARTED

New Jersey's total area is 8,722.58 square miles, of which 7,354.22 square miles are land area, and 1,368 .36 square miles is water area, making it the 47th state in terms of size.

Size figures from:

United States Summary: 2010, Population and Housing Unit Counts, 2010 Census of Population and Housing, United States Census Bureau, September 2012. Page 41.

****

When I began the project, Mark Di Ionno's *A Guide to New Jersey's Revolutionary War Trail* (New Brunswick, NJ: Rutgers University Press, 2000) was by far the most important book I had to help me locate Revolutionary War historic sites. About 300 of the 650 historic sites I ultimately visited and researched for the website were ones that I had originally discovered from Mark Di Ionno's book.

Other books which helped me locate some of New Jersey's Revolutionary War historic sites in the early days of the project include:

Craig Mitchell, *George Washington's New Jersey: A Guide to the Crossroads of the American Revolution* (Moorestown, NJ: Middle Atlantic Press, 2003)

Carol Karels, editor, *The Revolutionary War in Bergen County* (Charleston SC: The History Press, 2007)

Barbara Z. Marchant, editor, *Revolutionary Bergen County* (Charleston, SC: The History Press, 2009)

David C. Munn, *Battles and Skirmishes in New Jersey of the American Revolution*, (Bureau of Geology and Topography, Department of Environmental Protection, 1976)

Another book I would like to mention is Bart McDowell's *The Revolutionary War* (The National Geographic Society, 1967). It contains descriptions of Revolutionary War sites throughout many states, which the author visited with his family, including photos he took. This book did not specifically point me in the direction of any particular locations I would not have known about otherwise. But in hindsight, I think it was some kind of subtle inspiration for the project itself, even though I didn't realize it at the time.

CHAPTER 4 / HITTING THE ROAD

George Washington is known to have stayed at the John Holcombe House on two occasions: July 28-31, 1777 and June 21-22, 1778.

For details and accompanying source notes, see the page for Lambertville (in Hunterdon County) on the *Revolutionary War New Jersey* website.

****

The Flemington Raid occurred on December 14, 1776.

For details and accompanying source notes regarding the Flemington Raid, see the page for Flemington (in Hunterdon County) on the *Revolutionary War New Jersey* website.

CHAPTER 5 / NEW JERSEY WAR ZONE

Garret Durie's house still stands in Hillsdale, NJ.

For further details and accompanying source notes, see the page for Hillsdale (in Bergen County) on the *Revolutionary War New Jersey* website.

****

The location where Washington made the decision to head to Morristown after the Battle of Princeton is in Kingston, NJ.

For details and accompanying source notes, see the page for Kingston (in Somerset County) on the *Revolutionary War New Jersey* website.

****

For more details and accompanying source notes regarding the 1777 Morristown winter encampment, see the page for

Morristown (in Morris County) on the *Revolutionary War New Jersey* website.

CHAPTER 6 / EXPLORING THE STATE

Grave listings do exist for some older cemeteries, and can be found online, and in the collections of some libraries and historical societies. These can be especially helpful in cases where some original grave stones are missing, or have worn to the point of being unreadable.

The Find-A-Grave website (*https://www.findagrave.com*) is another tool for determining who is buried in a given cemetery. However, the information is incomplete, and sometimes inaccurate. Ultimately, I found the best way to verify that a grave is in a particular cemetery is to see it for yourself.

****

There are some Revolutionary War related houses in New Jersey which have been moved from their original locations. In these cases, the point about the angle of the sunlight would of course not apply. But in most cases, the houses are still in their original location.

CHAPTER 7 / MY FAVORITE TOWN

More information and accompanying source notes about Cranbury, its role in the Revolutionary War, and the Revolutionary War historic sites located there, can be found on the page for Cranbury (in Middlesex County) on the *Revolutionary War New Jersey* website.

CHAPTER 8 / CARS

The 1994 Oldsmobile I purchased from Paul not only made it through to the end of the *Revolutionary War New Jersey* project in 2017, but it continued to run until mid-2020. I junked it in early 2021.

CHAPTER 9 / THE PULASKI STATUE

The Pulaski statue in Wallington was sculpted by Mieczyslaw "Karol" Partyka (1958-2009), a Polish-born sculptor who immigrated to New York in 1989. The monument was dedicated October 4, 2002.

Sculptor credit and dedication date information from the plaque on the base of the statue.

Details about Partyka from:

• Irving Dejohn and Jonathan Lemire, "Polish-born Brooklyn Sculptor Karol Washes up on Nearby Beach After Working on Boat in Storm," *New York Daily News*, July 28, 2009.

• "A Retrospective Exhibition of Mieczyslaw "Karol" Partyka (1958-2009)," Consulate General of the Republic of Poland in New York, June 10, 2010.

****

Casimir Pulaski, who is remembered as the "Father of American Cavalry," did not survive the Revolutionary War. He died on October 11, 1779, from wounds suffered at the Battle of Savannah, Georgia.

CHAPTER 10 / THE HISTORY CONNECTION

The history books I read in my early twenties which first got me seriously interested in American history include: *Miracle at Philadelphia* by Catherine Drinker Bowen, Stephen E. Ambrose's three-volume biography of Richard Nixon, *The Autobiography of Malcolm X* by Malcolm X as told to Alex Haley, *Washington: The Indispensable Man* by James Thomas Flexner, and *Six Crises* by Richard Nixon.

My passion for all kinds of history then got a huge boost when I discovered the ten-part documentary series *The Day the Universe Changed*, by James Burke. I cannot overstate the impact that *The Day the Universe Changed* had on me and the way I think about history. I highly recommend it.

CHAPTER 11 / THE HARD WINTER

The 1777 encampment was described in Chapter 5.

****

Joseph Plumb Martin quote from:
Joseph Plumb Martin, Edited by George F. Scheer, *Private Yankee Doodle* (Eastern National, 2012 Edition) Pages 170 and 172.

****

For more details about the weather during the winter of 1779-1780, see:

David M. Ludlum, *Early American Winters 1604 - 1820 (Volume I)* (Boston: American Meteorological Society, 1966) Pages 111 – 133.

****

For more details and accompanying source notes regarding the 1779-1780 Morristown winter encampment, see the page for Morristown (in Morris County) on the *Revolutionary War New Jersey* website.

CHAPTER 12 / A SENSE OF PLACE

No Chapter Notes

CHAPTER 13 / THE HELICOPTER INCIDENT

No Chapter Notes

CHAPTER 14 / A MORE DISTANT PAST

James McHenry quote from:

Bernard C. Steiner, *The Life and Correspondence of James McHenry* (Cleveland: The Burrows Brothers Company, 1907) Pages 21-22.

****

The time frames listed for the age of the earth, the existence of human beings, and recorded history are standard numbers found in a number of reference works.

****

For more details and accompanying source notes regarding the Paterson Great Falls, see the page for Paterson (in Passaic County) on the *Revolutionary War New Jersey* website.

CHAPTER 15 / THE PROJECT GROWS

No Chapter Notes

CHAPTER 16 / GOING TO THE SOURCE

The Founder's Online website is at *https://founders.archives.gov/*

CHAPTER 17 / A SORROWFUL PAST

The writings of Stephen E. Ambrose influenced my observations that those of us who have not been in combat can never fully understand the experience of combat soldiers — in particular, several paragraphs that Ambrose wrote in his essay "My Lai, Atrocities in Historical Perspective," which is included in his 1997 book *Americans at War* (Jacksonville, MS: University Press of Mississippi).

****

Nicholas Collin's journal excerpt from:

Nicholas Collin, Amandus Johnson, *The Journal and Biography of Nicholas Collin 1746-1831* (Philadelphia: The New Jersey Society of Pennsylvania, 1936) Page 246.

For more information and accompanying source notes about Reverend Nicholas Collin, see the page for Swedesboro (in Gloucester County) on the *Revolutionary War New Jersey* website.

****

Excerpts from Jemima Condict's diary from:

Jemima Condict, *Jemima Condict, Her Book: Being a Transcript of the Diary of an Essex County Maid During the Revolutionary War* (Newark: The Carteret Book Club, 1930) Pages 59-64.

This book was published in a limited edition of only 200 copies (as stated on the last page of the book), and so it is very difficult to locate a copy. One of the surviving copies is in the collection of the John Cotton Dana Library at Rutgers University - The State University of New Jersey in Newark. I was able to make photocopies of the entire book while visiting the library.

Some excerpts of Jemima Condict's diary appeared in the following books:

Elizabeth Evans, *Weathering the Storm / Women of the American Revolution* (New York: Charles Scribner's Sons, 1975). (Note that in the quotations from Jemima Condict's diary in this book, Jemima's spelling, grammar, and punctuation are corrected and modernized.)

June Sprigg, *Domestick Beings* (New York: Alfred A. Knopf, 1984)

****

For more information and accompanying source notes about Jemima Condict, see the pages for Orange and Bloomfield (both in Essex County) on the *Revolutionary War New Jersey* website.

CHAPTER 18 / STAY HUMBLE

No Chapter Notes

CHAPTER 19 / AN IMPERFECT PAST

Much of my research with Revolutionary War era newspaper items utilized:
Archives of the State of New Jersey, Second Series, Vol I-V (Documents Relating to the Revolutionary History of the State of New Jersey / Extracts from American Newspapers relating to New Jersey)
Published 1901-1917.

CHAPTER 20 / RESEARCH DAYS – GOOD AND BAD

The Name Game subheading takes its name from the 1964 Shirley Ellis song of the same name, which she co-wrote with Lincoln Chase.

CHAPTER 21 / PICK A CARD, ANY CARD

No Chapter Notes

CHAPTER 22 / WASHINGTON'S FOOTSTEPS

For more information and accompanying source notes about some of the Washington-related sites mentioned in this chapter, see the pages for Hopewell Township (in Mercer County), Kingston (in Somerset County), Lambertville (in Hunterdon County), Nutley (in Essex County), and Trenton (in Mercer County) on the *Revolutionary War New Jersey* website.

CHAPTER 23 / A DAY IN THE LIFE

The title of this chapter is of course an homage to the song of the same name by the greatest band in the history of the universe, which appeared on their 1967 *Sgt. Pepper's Lonely Hearts Club Band* LP. (Lennon-McCartney)

CHAPTER 24 / JERSEY

The "a hundred-mile stretch between New York and Phila-delphia" quote is from:

Richard Brookhiser, *Founding Father: Rediscovering George Washington* (New York: The Free Press, 1996) page 25.

****

The *All in the Family* episode described and quoted is "Mike Makes His Move," Season 5, Episode 24. It originally aired on March 8, 1975.

Archie portrayed by Carroll O'Connor. Mike portrayed by Rob Reiner.

Teleplay by Lou Derman & Bill Davenport. Story by Lou Derman & Bill Davenport and Robert Arnott.

(Writing credits appear on screen at the end of the episode.)

CHAPTER 25 / 2014

No Chapter Notes

CHAPTER 26 / IRON ORE NOT

I would like to point out that while I really hated working on iron related topics, there were sometimes non-iron stories associated with the iron locations which were of some interest.

I would further like to point out that I did have one enjoyable time while researching iron production. During my research for the Long Pond Iron Works in West Milford, I interviewed Joe Rosolen, Vice President of the Friends of Long Pond Ironworks. I have known Joe for many years, and so it was a pleasure to talk with him, even if we were talking about iron!

CHAPTER 27 / JUST KEEP MOVING

For more information and accompanying source notes about the locations we visited that day, the Hamburg Baptist Church Cemetery and the site of Joseph Sharp's Iron Works, see the page for Hamburg (in Sussex County) on the *Revolutionary War New Jersey* website.

CHAPTER 28 / STOP AND LOOK AROUND

For more information and accompanying source notes regarding the Battle of Turtle Gut Inlet, see the page for Wildwood Crest (in Cape May County) on the *Revolutionary War New Jersey* website.

For more information about artist Illia Barger, see her website *https://www.illiabarger.com/*

Each of the public art pieces listed on the chart is shown and described on the appropriate town pages of the *Revolutionary War New Jersey* website.

CHAPTER 29 / THE DINNER QUESTION

The following information was provided to me by Samantha Snyder, Access Services Librarian, The Fred W. Smith National Library for the Study of George Washington, Mount Vernon Ladies' Association, in an email exchange on January 8, 2019:

> *"We don't have any definitive evidence that Billy Lee could read, it was certainly a possibility. Billy often*

delivered and picked up the family's mail at the Alexandria Post Office, so it might have been handy, if he could make sure that he had the correct mail.

"In regard to Billy 'organizing' the General's papers, we know that he was in charge of seeing that the trunks carrying the papers were safe and not left behind, when the army changed locations. There is no evidence that he was acting as a secretary or archivist. We have no papers that were thought to have been written by Billy Lee."

CHAPTER 30 / THE PRESSURE BUILDS

No Chapter Notes

CHAPTER 31 / 2016 – THE FIRST HALF

"Seasons in the Sun" by Terry Jacks was released in 1973, and contains lyrics like "Goodbye my friend it's hard to die; When all the birds are singing in the sky."

"Seasons in the Sun" is based on the 1961 French-language song **Le Moribond** by Jacques Brel with new English lyrics by Rod McKuen. Its writing credits are therefore Brel-McKuen.

CHAPTER 32 / BENJAMIN FRANKLIN'S NEW JERSEY

Biographical details of Benjamin Franklin's life were drawn mainly from:

- Walter Isaacson, **Benjamin Franklin, An American Life** (New York: Simon & Schuster, 2003)
- Benjamin Franklin, **The Autobiography of Benjamin Franklin**

****

More information and accompanying source notes regarding the Franklin-related locations mentioned in this chapter can be found on the pages for Burlington (in Burlington County), Perth Amboy (in Middlesex County), and Piscataway (in Middlesex County) on the *Revolutionary War New Jersey* website.

****

Quote from John Adams Diary:
"[Monday September 9, 1776.] ," *Founders Online,* National Archives, https://founders.archives.gov/documents/Adams/01-03-02-0016-0187. [Original source: *The Adams Papers*, Diary and Autobiography of John Adams, vol. 3, *Diary, 1782–1804; Autobiography, Part One to October 1776*, ed. L. H. Butterfield. Cambridge, MA: Harvard University Press, 1961, pp. 417–420.]

CHAPTER 33 / GREAT MONTH / SAD DAY

Although there were a number of times the Oldsmobile needed repairs during the years I was working on the project, this was the only time it actually broke down while I was out on a *Revolutionary War New Jersey* drive.

****

How I came to own the Oldsmobile which had previously belonged to Paul's mother is explained in Chapter 8, "Cars".

CHAPTER 34 / 2016 – THE SECOND HALF

"In the Year 2525 (Exordium & Terminus)" was released in 1968 by Zager and Evans. Written by Rick Evans.

"Getting Closer" was released in 1979 by Wings on their *Back to the Egg* LP. Written by Paul McCartney.

CHAPTER 35 / GETTING VERY NEAR THE END

The title of this chapter is another reference to a Beatles song, in this case drawn from the lyrics of the song, "Sgt. Pepper's Lonely Hearts Club Band (Reprise)" from the 1967 album, *Sgt. Pepper's Lonely Hearts Club Band*. (Lennon-McCartney)

****

For more information and accompanying source notes about the Kingsland Manor, see the page for Nutley (in Essex County) on the *Revolutionary War New Jersey* website.

CHAPTER 36 / THE LAST DAY

Joan Barrett originally contacted me in 2012. Joan was doing research about her great-great-great-great-great-grandfather Jesse Dolbeer, who served in the Middlesex County militia during the Revolutionary War. She discovered my website and asked me some questions that pertained to her research. We remained in contact after our discussions about Jesse Dolbeer. Joan had previously been a teacher, and at some point she offered to do final proofreads for my website.

Jesse Dolbeer had a house in Plainfield, which was sadly demolished on June 14, 2016, and another house in Scotch Plains, which still stands.

For more information and accompanying source notes regarding Jesse Dolbeer and the two houses, see the pages for Plainfield and Scotch Plains (both in Union County) on the *Revolutionary War New Jersey* website.

****

I am of the generation that grew up with the *Planets of the Apes* craze of the early 1970's, which then meant the original five films (released between 1968 and 1973), and the TV show which ran for only fourteen episodes in 1974. It is the earliest specific thing in my life I can recall taking a big interest in. While I still have great nostalgia and affection for those original *Planet of the Apes* films and TV show, I do not have an interest in the films made in the 21st century under that name.

One of the astronauts on the TV show (Pete Burke, portrayed by James Naughton) is supposed to be from New Jersey. In the first episode, "Escape From Tomorrow," he states:

"I was just thinking, when I was a kid in Jersey City, I couldn't even see the stars. Used to dream about 'em though. Used to dream about being up there with 'em."

Written by Art Wallace.

(Writing credit appears on screen at the beginning of the episode.)

CHAPTER 37 / AFTER THE END

The title of this chapter bookends the *Citizen Kane* reference of the title of Chapter Two "Before The Beginning."

****

Rod Serling (1924-1975) was born in Syracuse, NY, but grew up in Binghamton, NY after his family moved there. He was the creator of the *Twilight Zone* TV show, which ran for five seasons from 1959-1964, and he wrote 92 of its 156 episodes. Before working on the *Twilight Zone*, Serling made his name as a writer for live TV. Two of his most well-known scripts of that period were *Patterns* and *Requiem for a Heavyweight*. Among his other credits are the screenplays for *Seven Days in May*, which is one of my favorite films, and the first *Planet of the Apes* film (which is co-credited to Michael Wilson.)

I first saw an episode of the *Twilight Zone* nearly four decades ago, and immediately felt a connection to it. My love, esteem, and respect for the show has only grown over time.

There have been a number of remakes of the *Twilight Zone* since Serling's death, but other than the 1983 feature film which I saw as a teenager, I have never watched any of them, and have no desire to. The *Twilight Zone* is not the *Twilight Zone* without Rod Serling, and the fact that others might acquire the legal right to use the show's name does not change that.

****

Once I settled on the idea that this book would be a combination of my own experiences and historical stories, there were three books I had read in the past which provided some inspiration for the format:

Billy Bryson, *A Walk in the Woods* (New York: Broadway Books, 1998)

Bob Thompson, *Born on a Mountaintop: On the Road with Davy Crockett and the Ghosts of the Wild Frontier* (New York: Crown Publishing Group, 2013)

Stephen E. Ambrose, *To America* (New York: Simon & Schuster, 2002)

****

My great-aunt Stephanie Evans was born Stephanie Czechowicz in New Jersey in 1910. She was my grandfather's younger sister. She married Adam Evans in 1941. At the time she acquired the Royal Quiet Deluxe typewriter, she was most likely doing administrative work for her husband's engineering company. She died in 2000 in St. Louis at age 90.

(This information was provided to me by Stephanie's stepson Arnold Evans.)

****

At one point towards the end of writing the book, the draw band of the *Royal Quiet Deluxe* manual typewriter broke. My friend Michele Marra loaned me a *Sears Electric 1* electric typewriter (manufactured in 1974 or 1975), which allowed me to keep writing. Several weeks later, I had my *Royal Quiet Deluxe* repaired by Albert Kren of Princeton, who has been repairing typewriters there since the mid-fifties.

ABOUT THE AUTHOR

Al Frazza is a proud lifelong resident of North Jersey, who has had a passion for history for much of his life. He is the creator of the *RevolutionaryWarNewJersey.com* website, which is used by thousands of people every week to help them explore New Jersey's Revolutionary War historic sites.

Al's history work and photographs have been featured in a variety of New Jersey publications, including *The Star-Ledger, New Jersey Monthly, Passaic Valley Today, The Sparta Independent, The River View Observer, The Home News Tribune, The Courier News, The New Jersey Herald, The Advertiser-News, The Township Journal, The Atlantic Highlands Herald, Beverly Bee*, and *The Hunterdon Review*. In 2018, Al received the History Award from the Chinkchewunska Chapter of the Daughters of the American Revolution, "in recognition of his outstanding dedication to the preservation and sharing of New Jersey History."

When he is not busy researching and writing, Al tries to fit in as much time as possible listening to Beatles records, watching classic films, and enjoying life with his fiancée Toni.

This is his first book.

www.revolutionarywarnewjersey.com   www.alfrazza.com